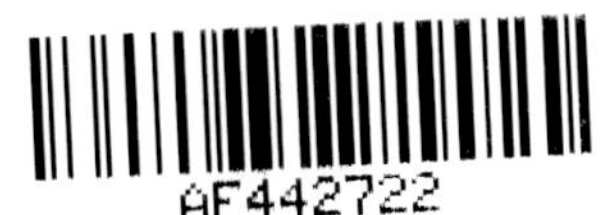

BEAUTIFUL
FLOWER DESIGNS

HUE COLORING

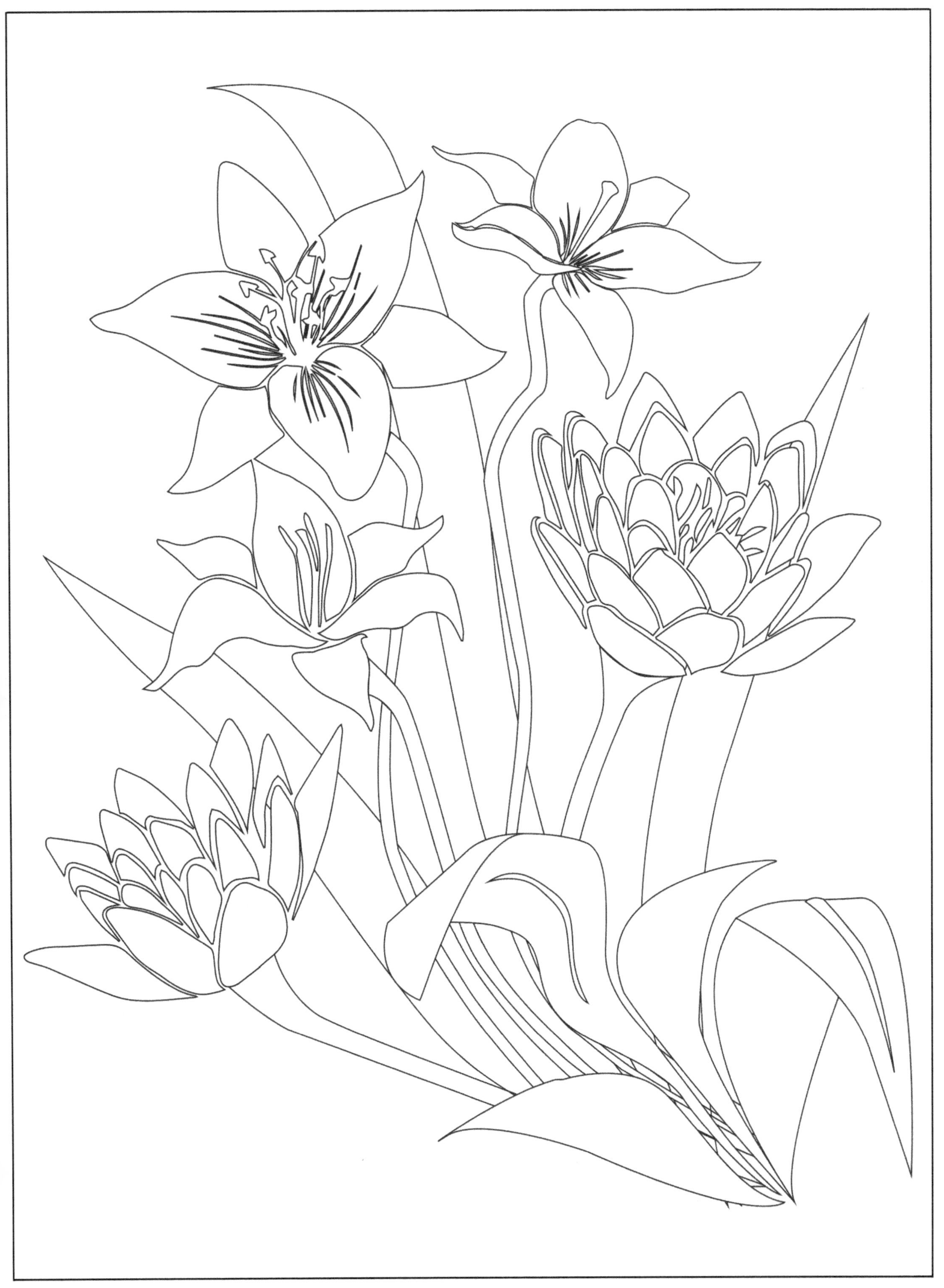

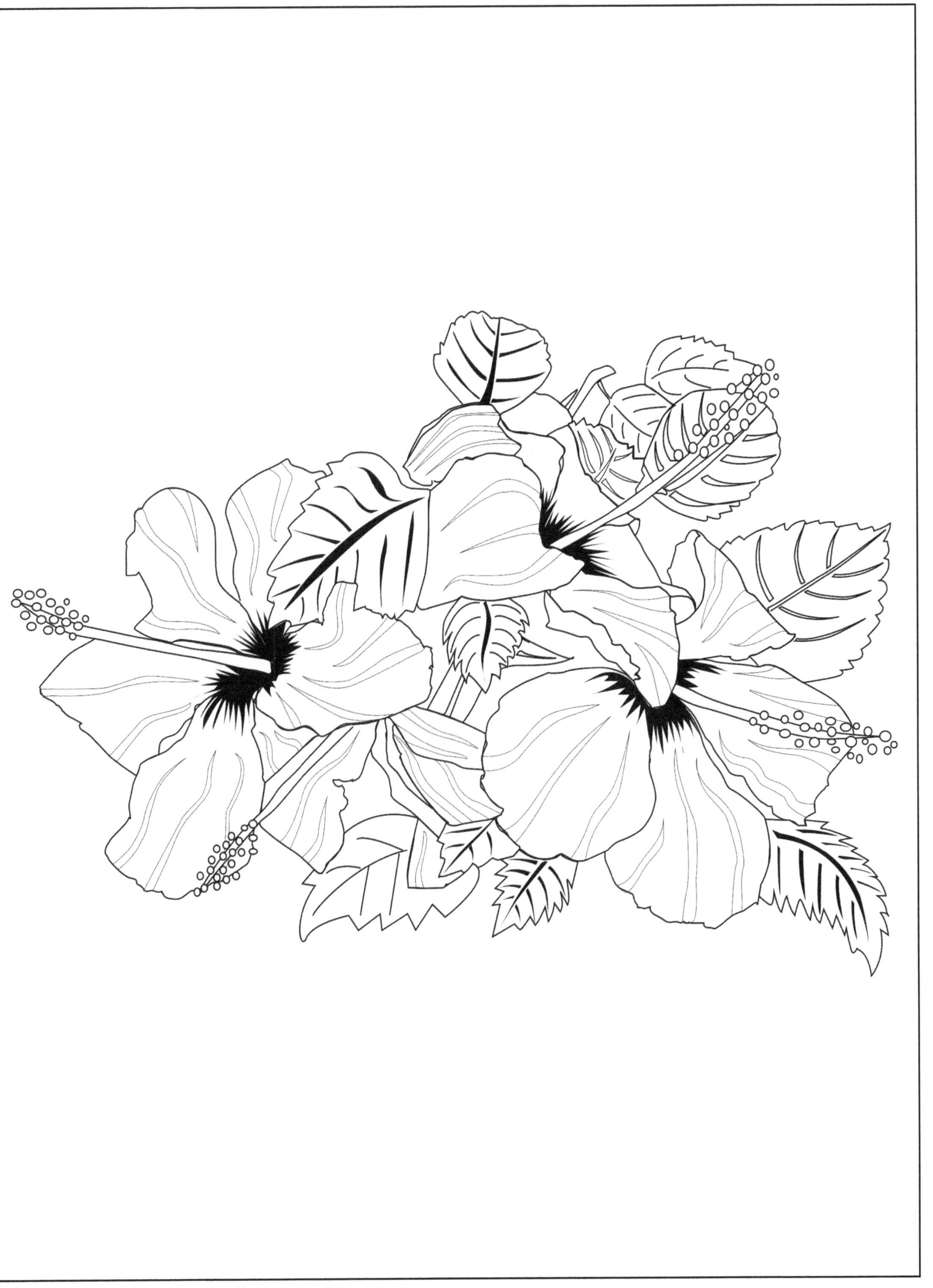

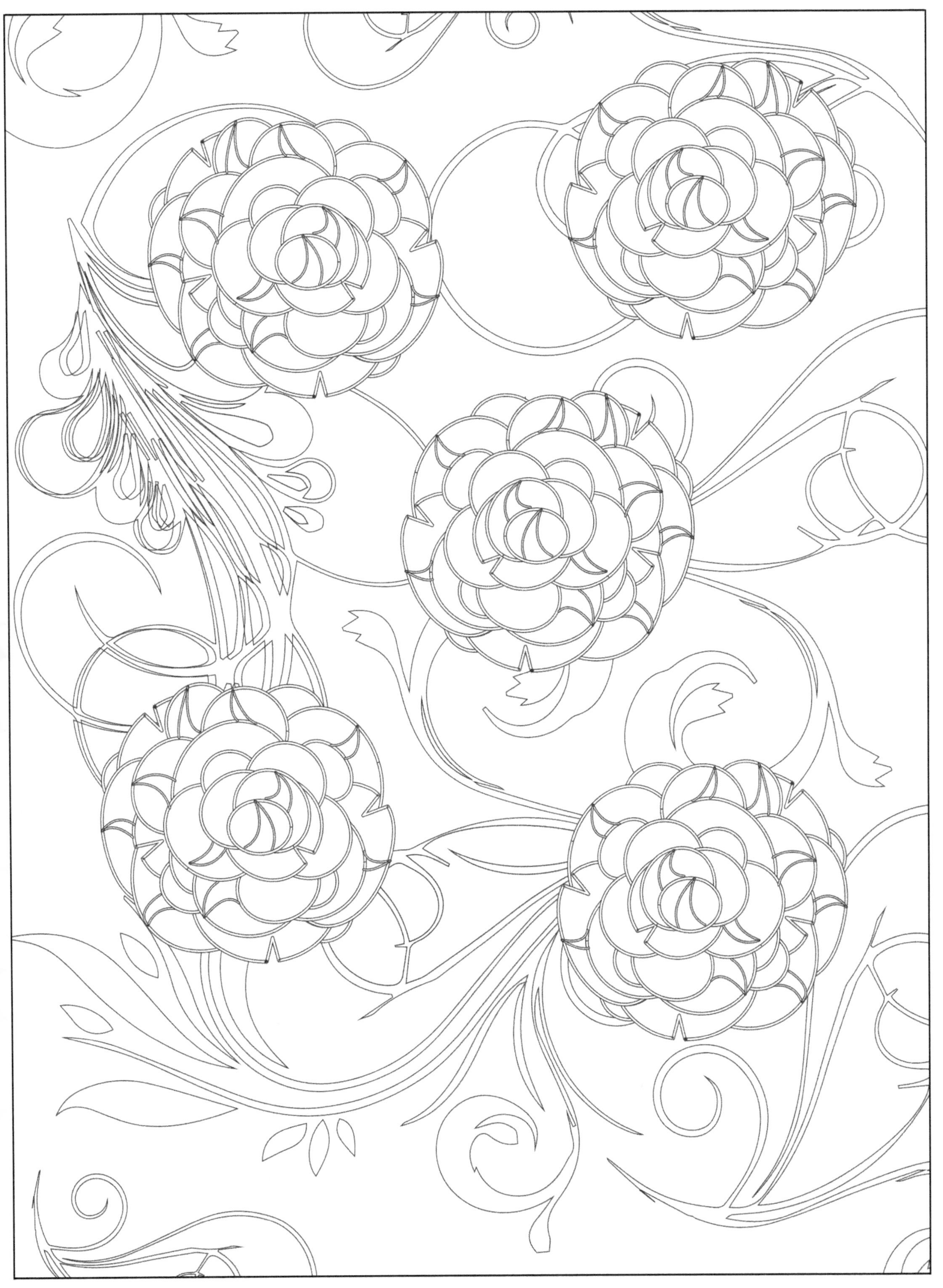

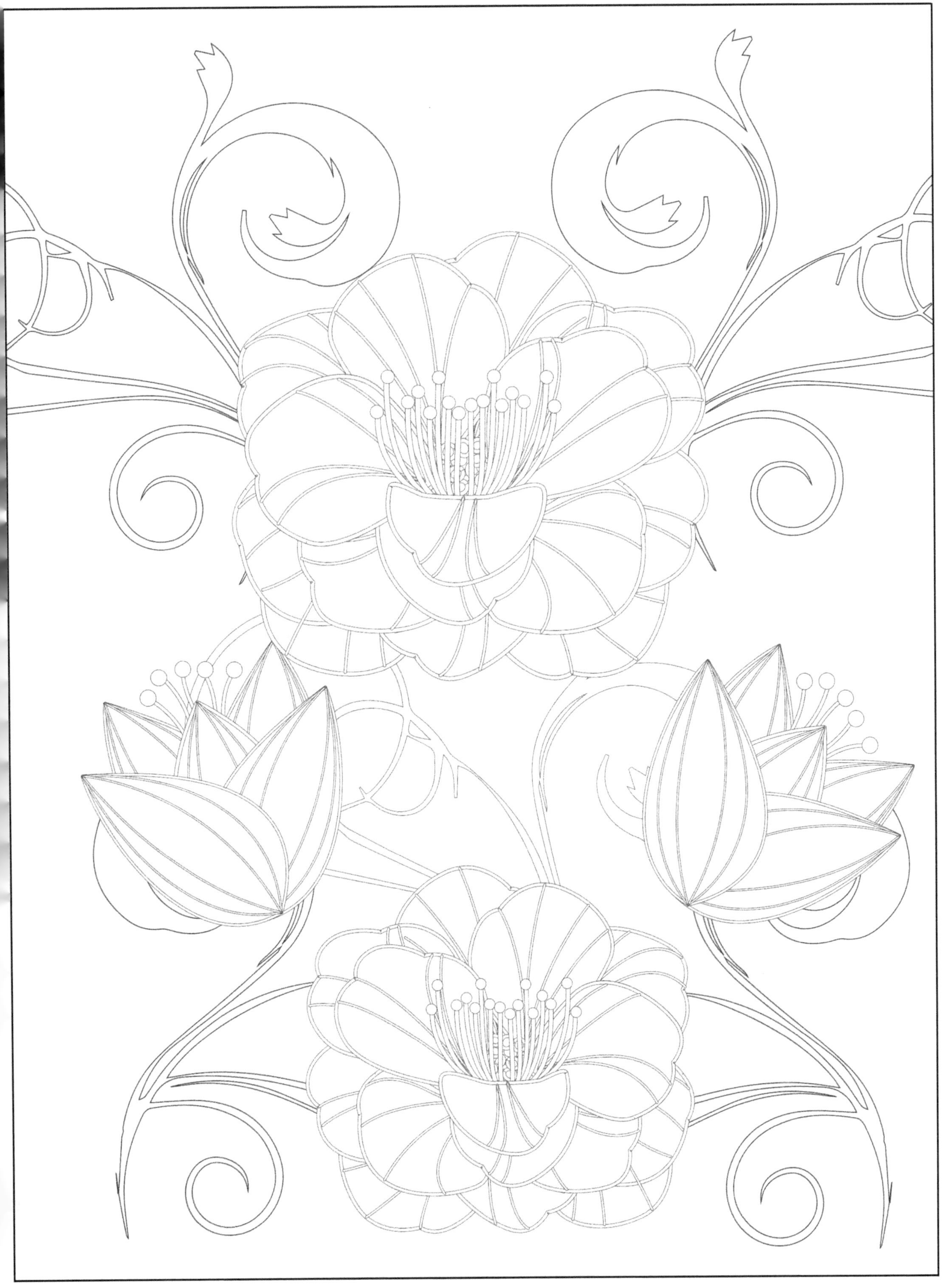

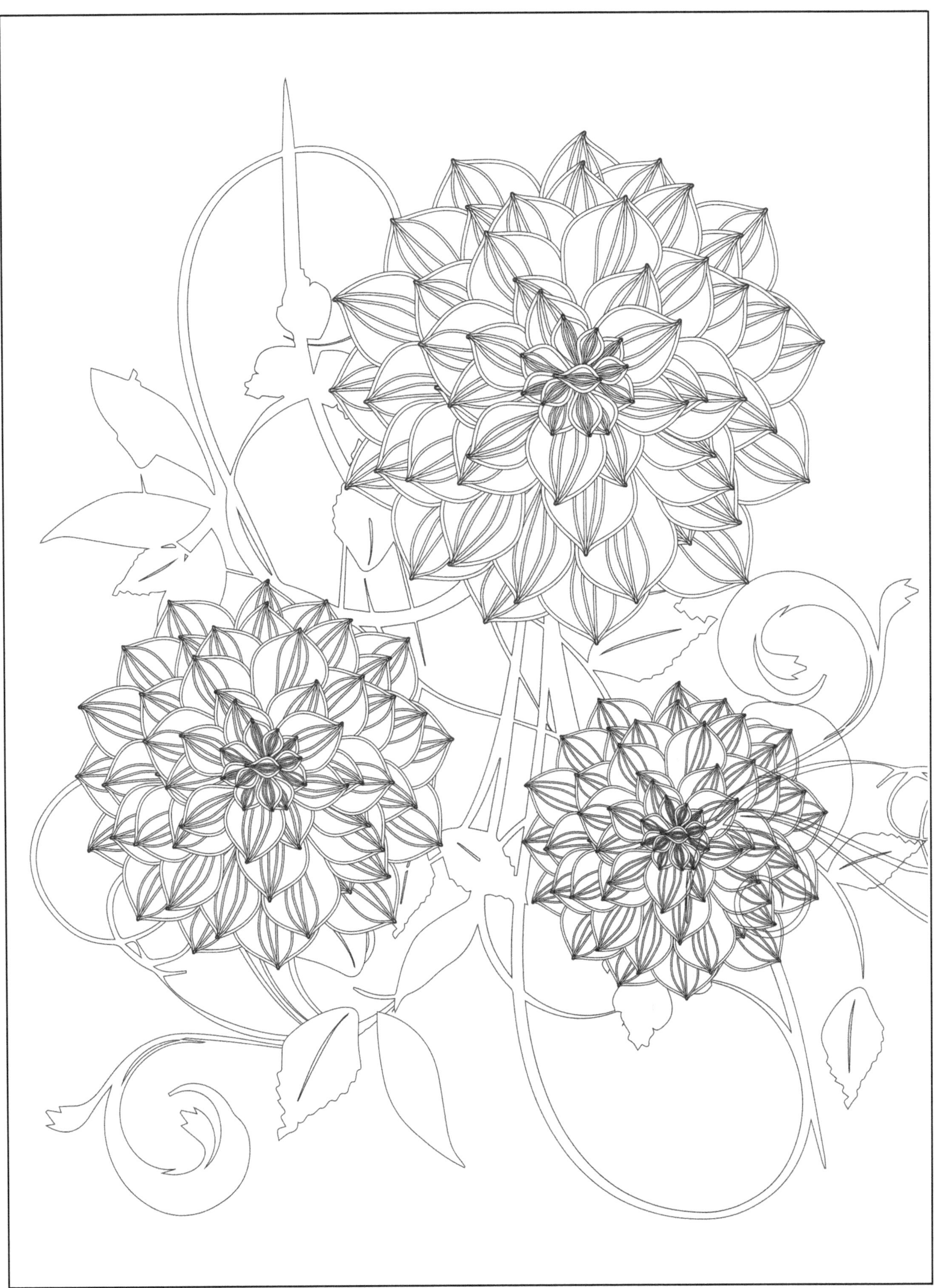

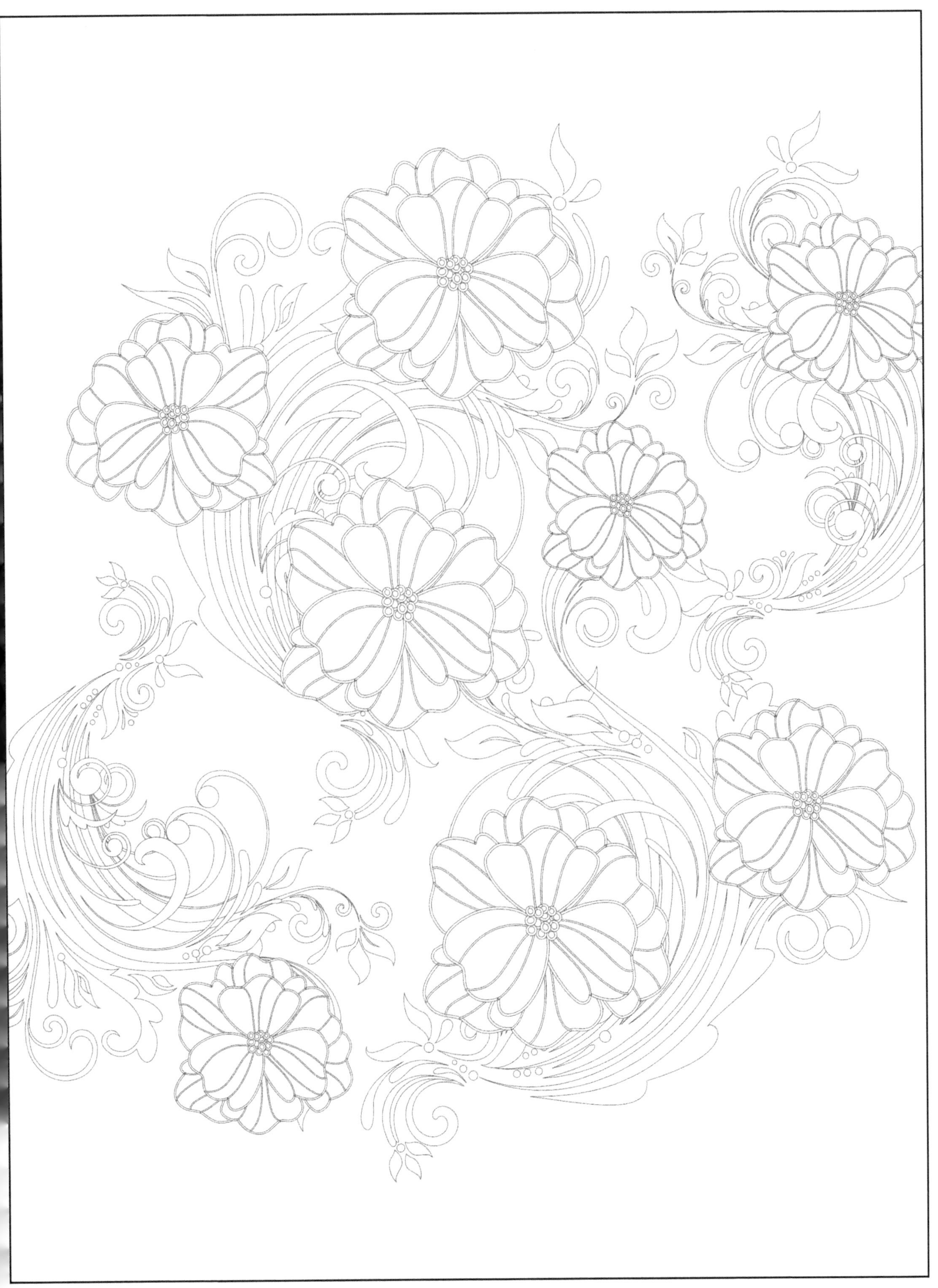

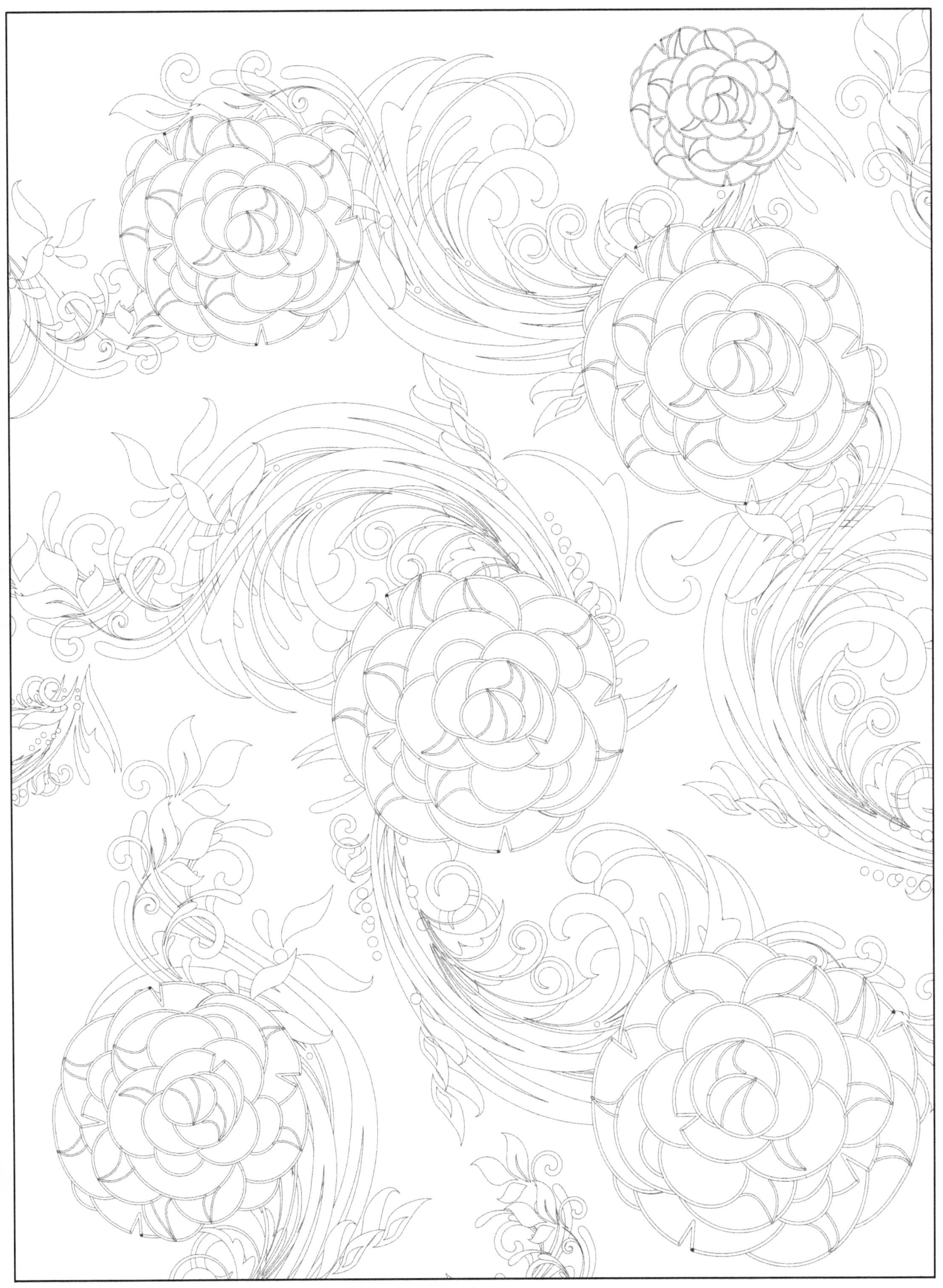

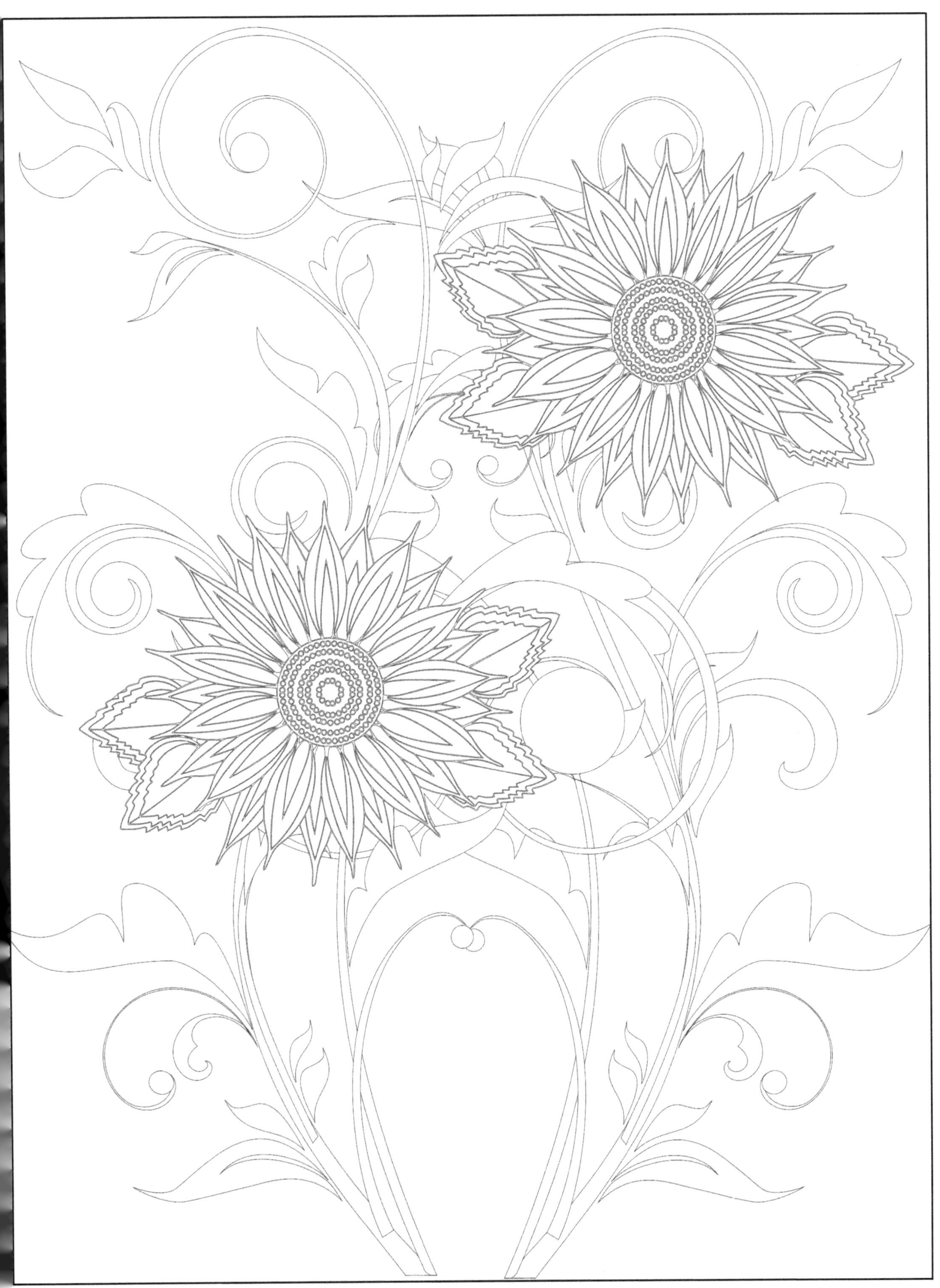

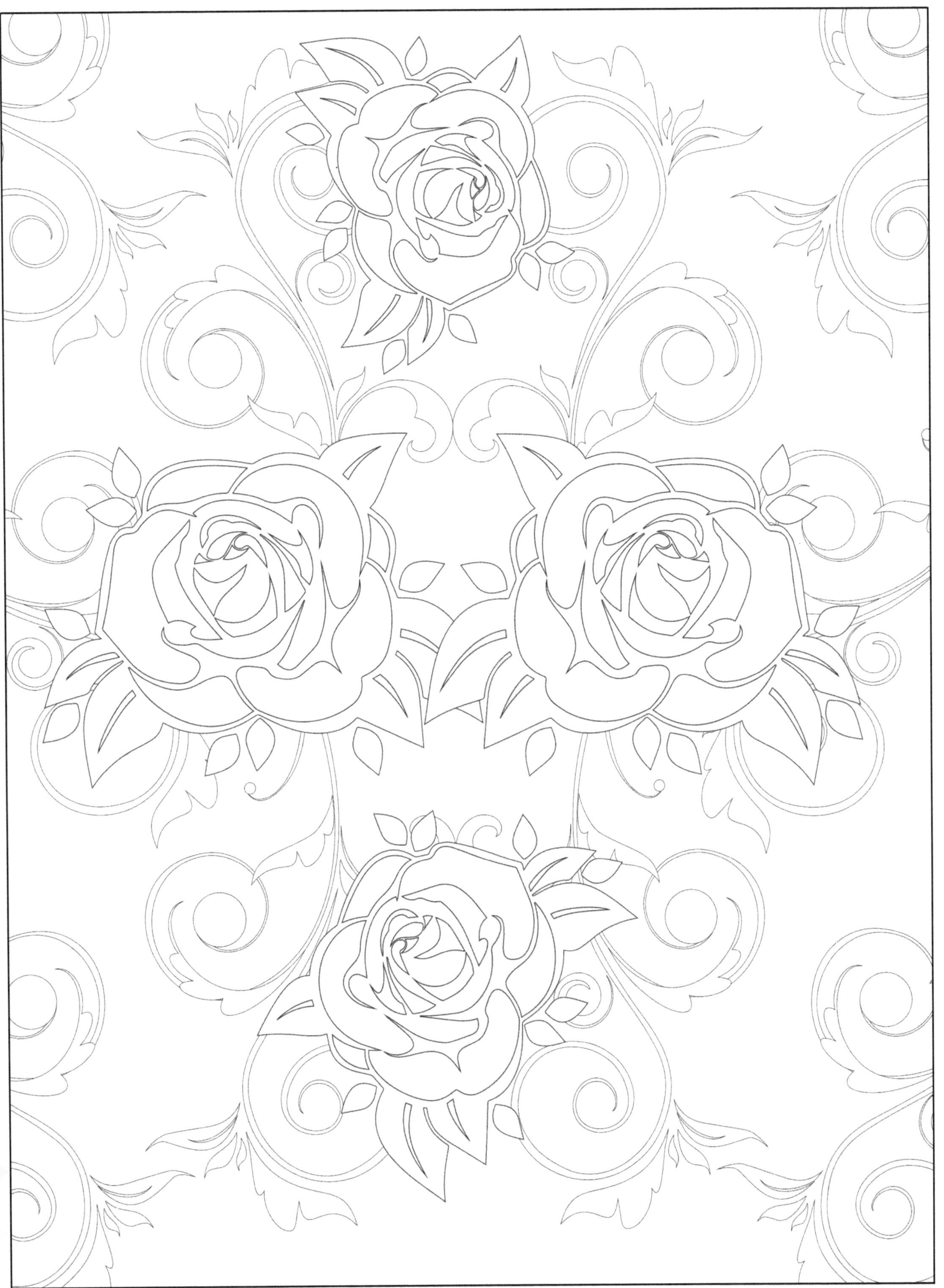

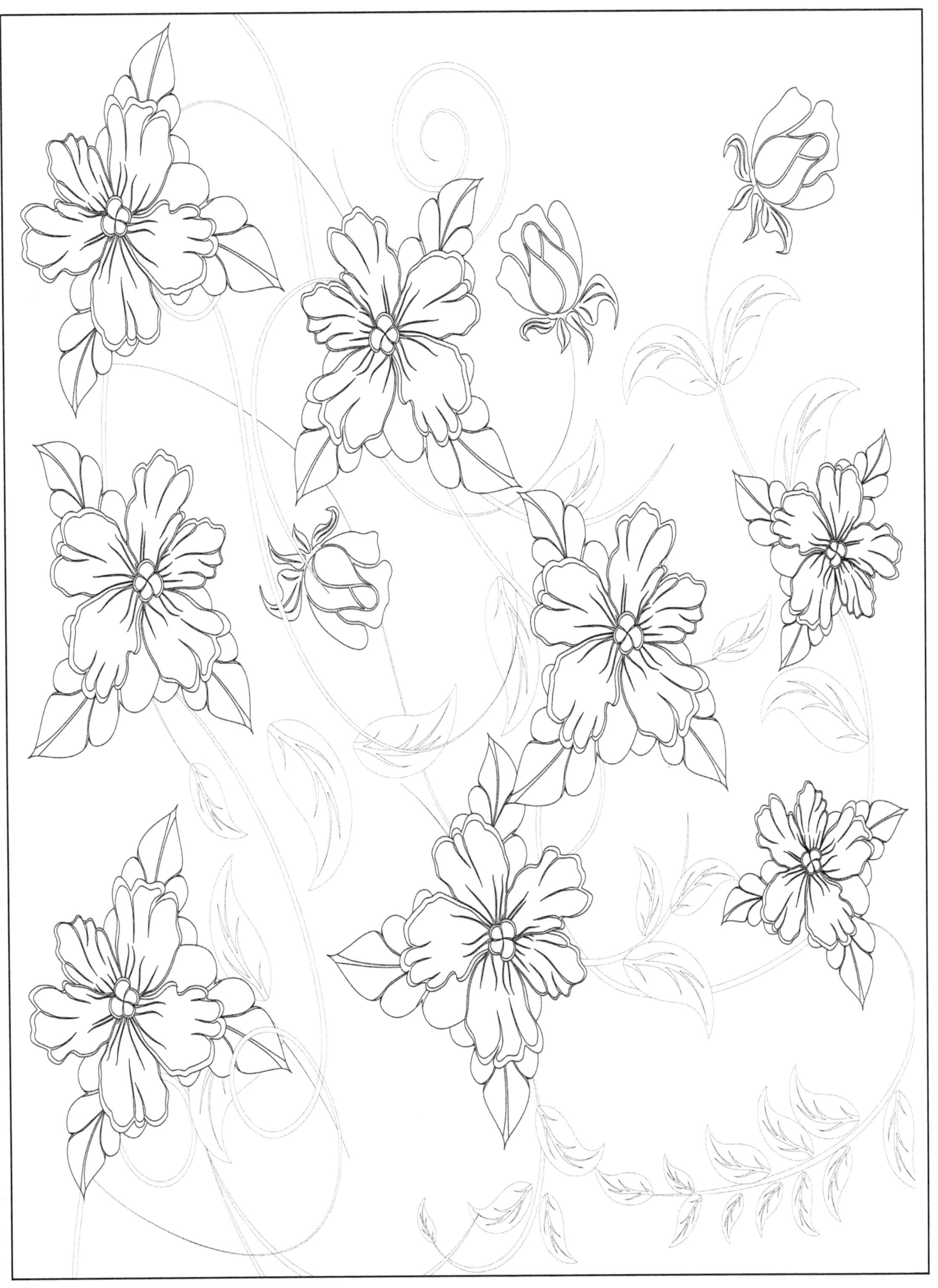

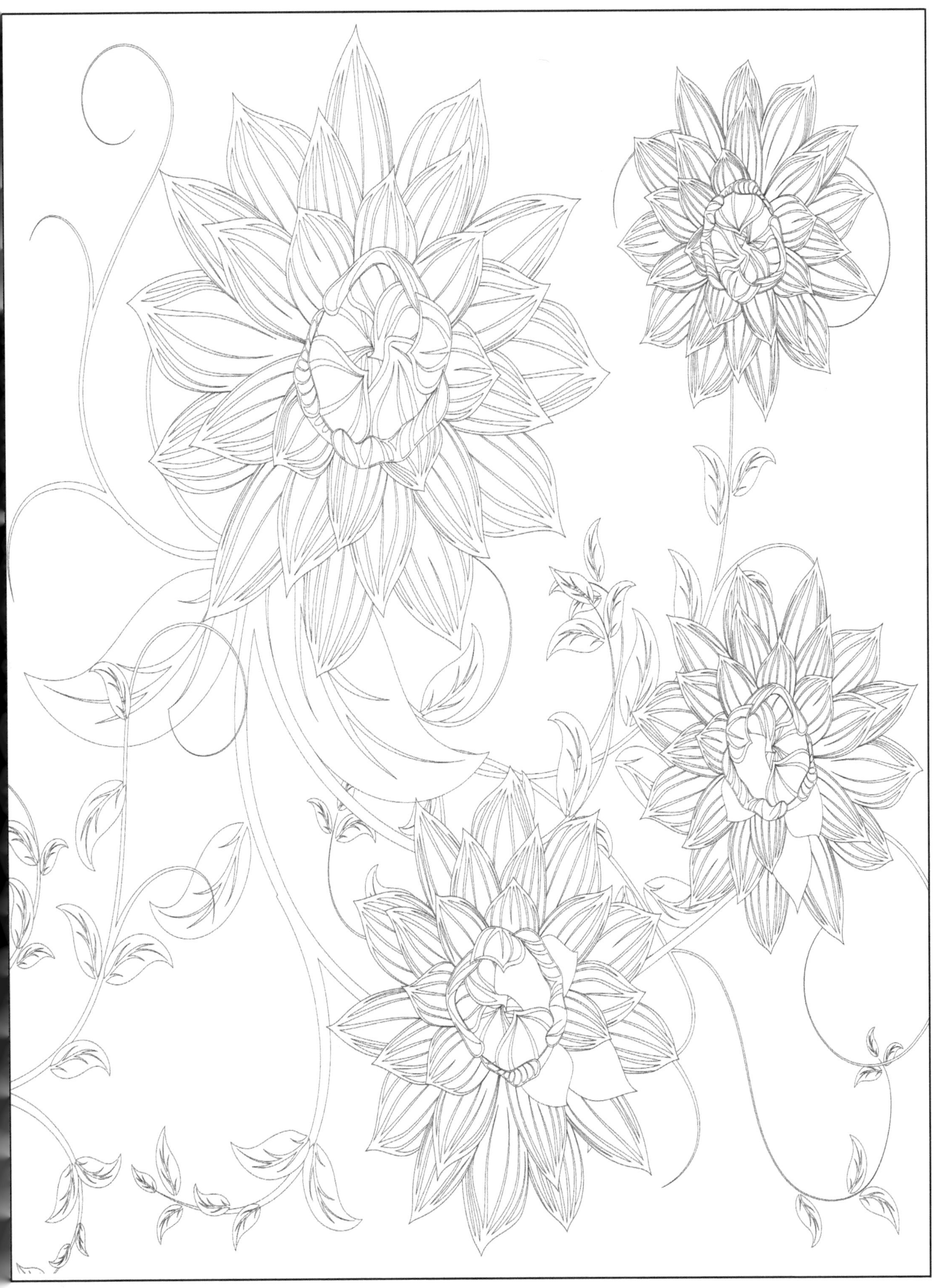

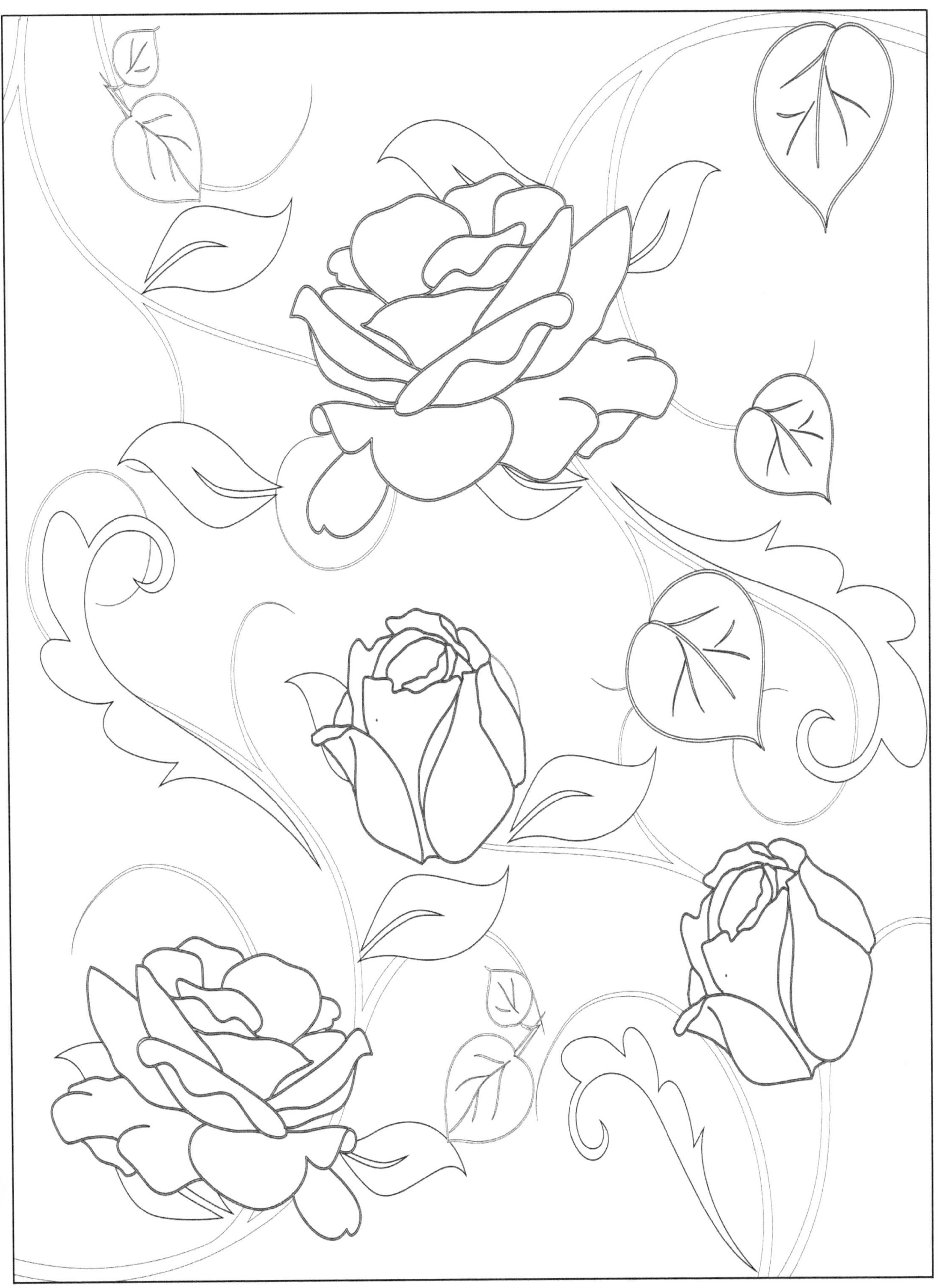

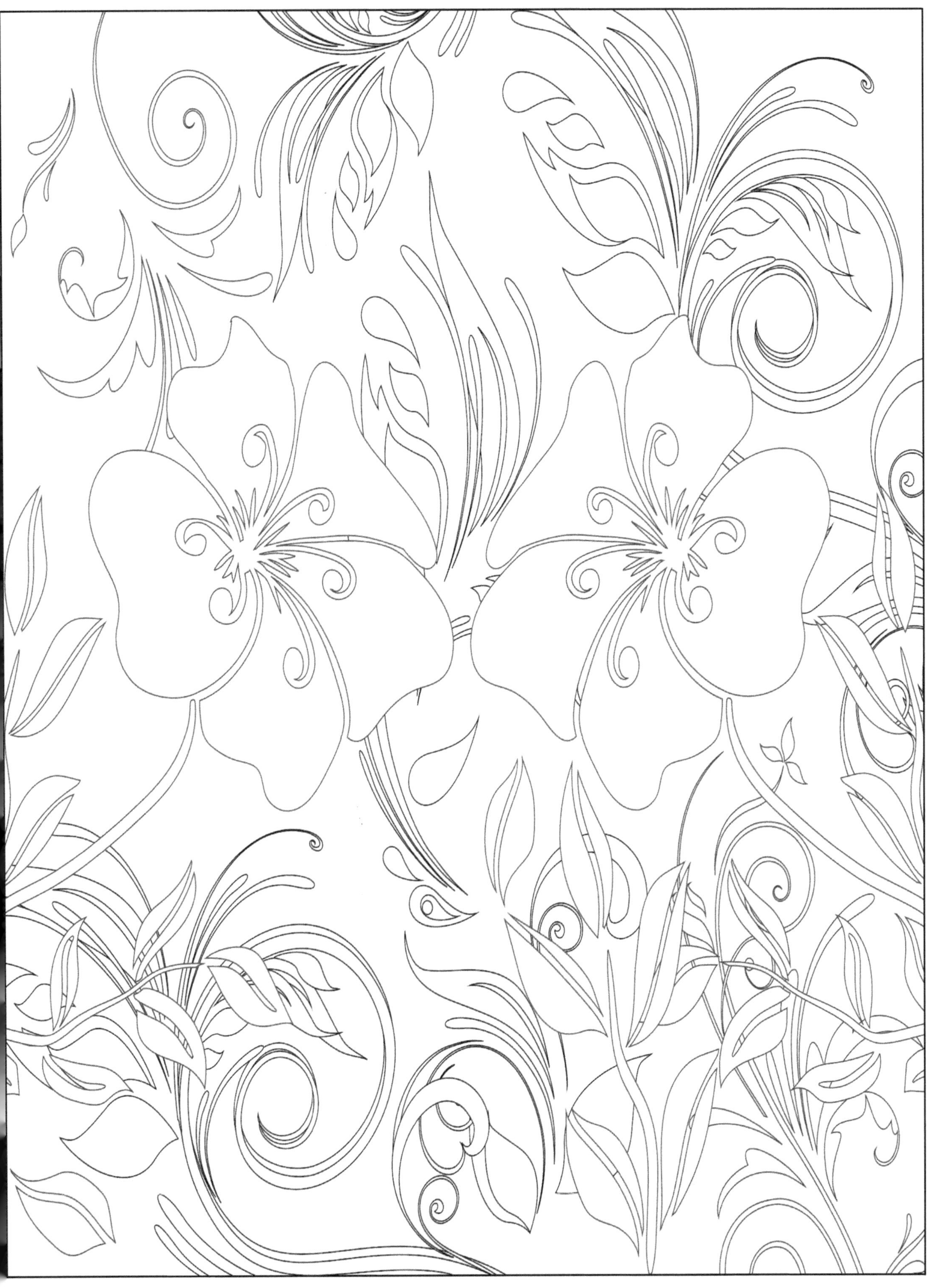

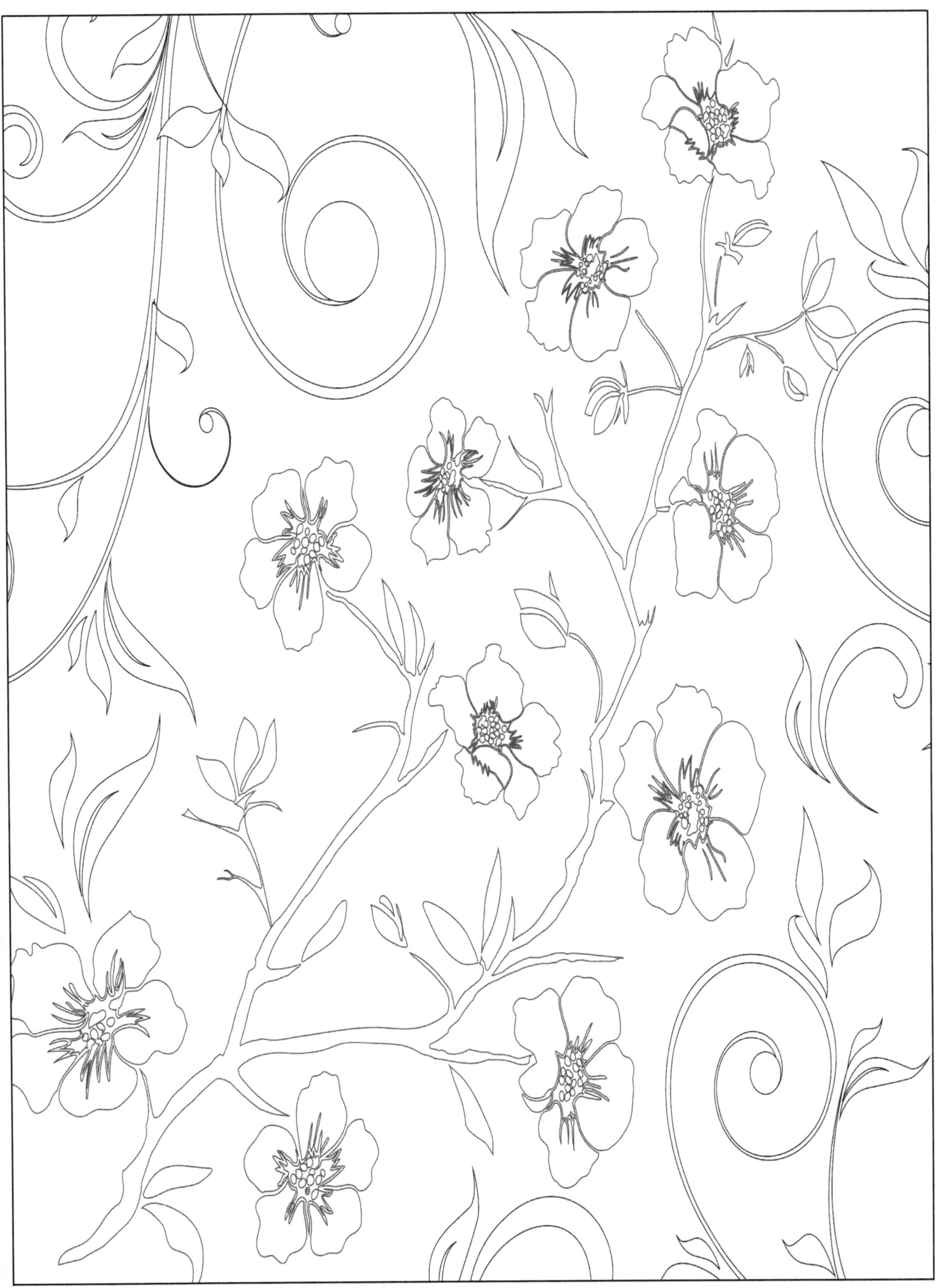

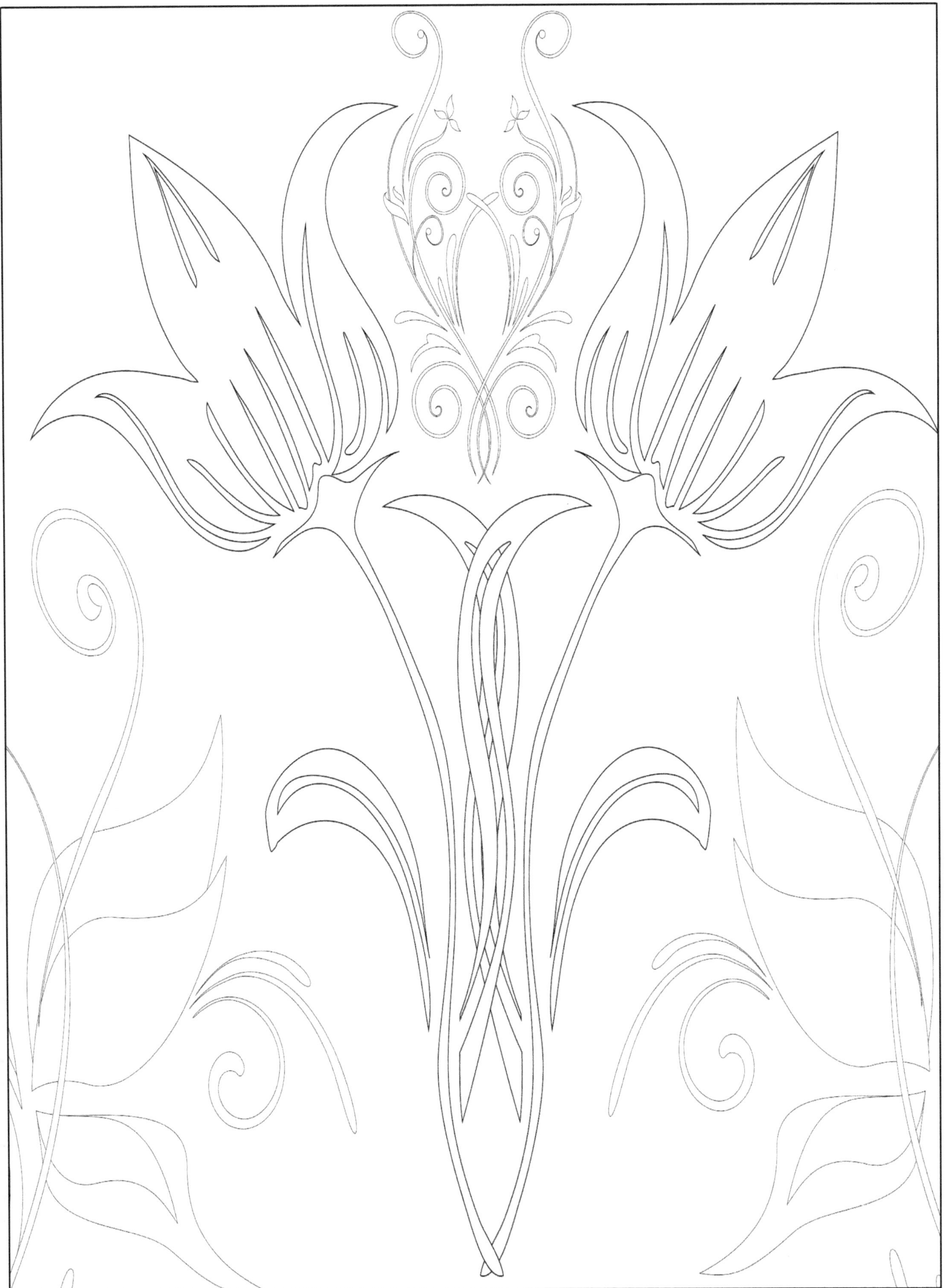

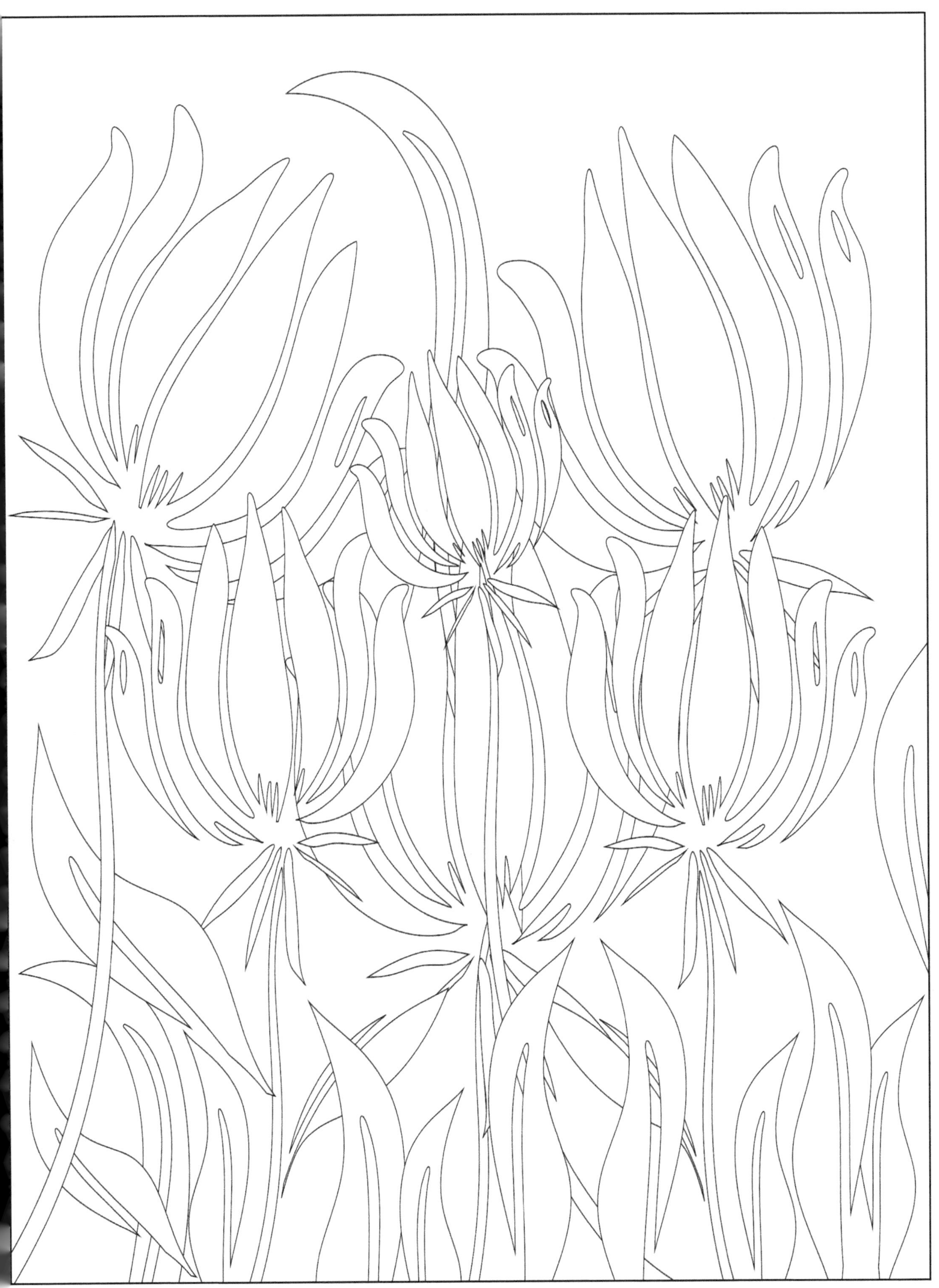

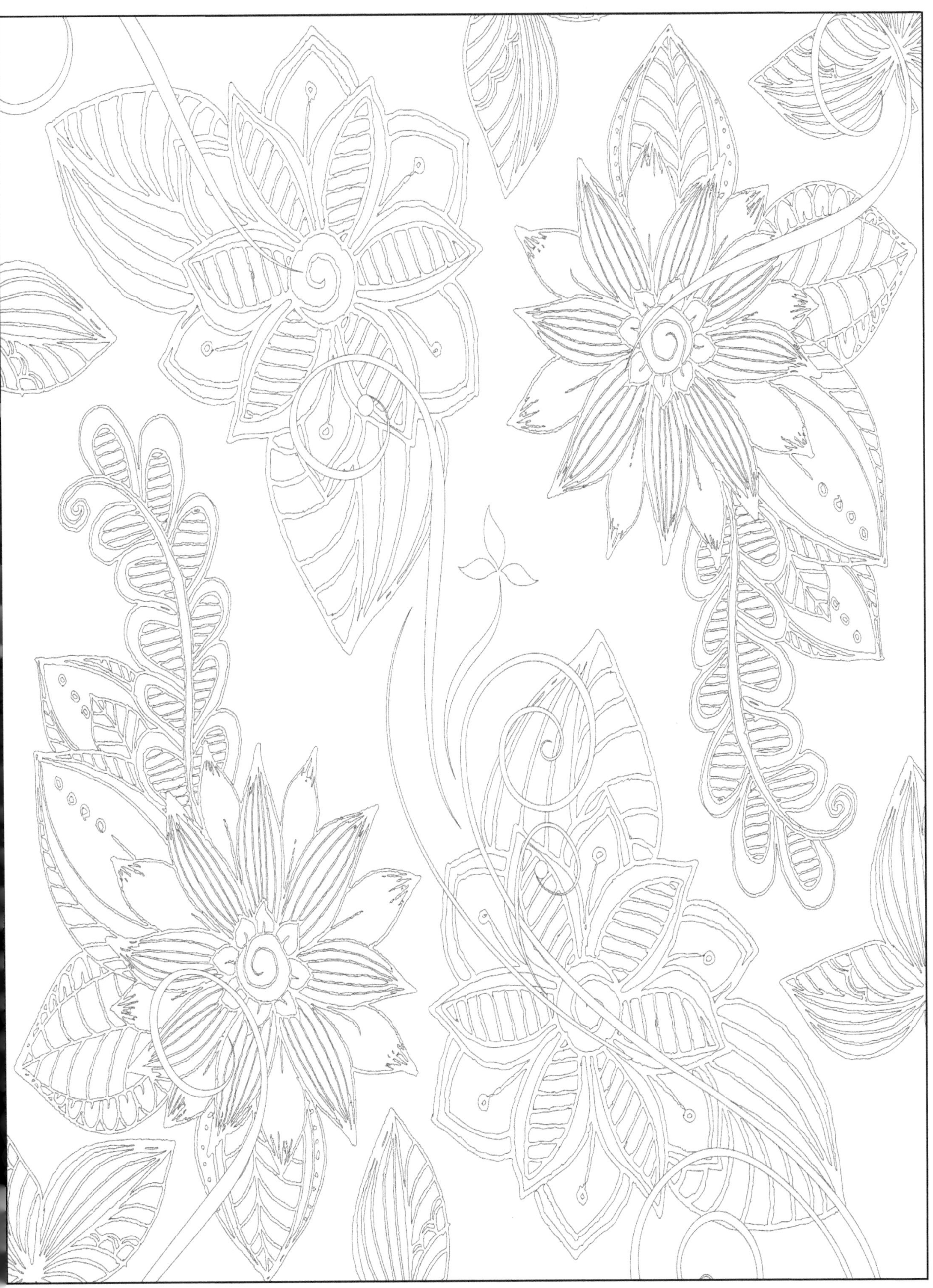

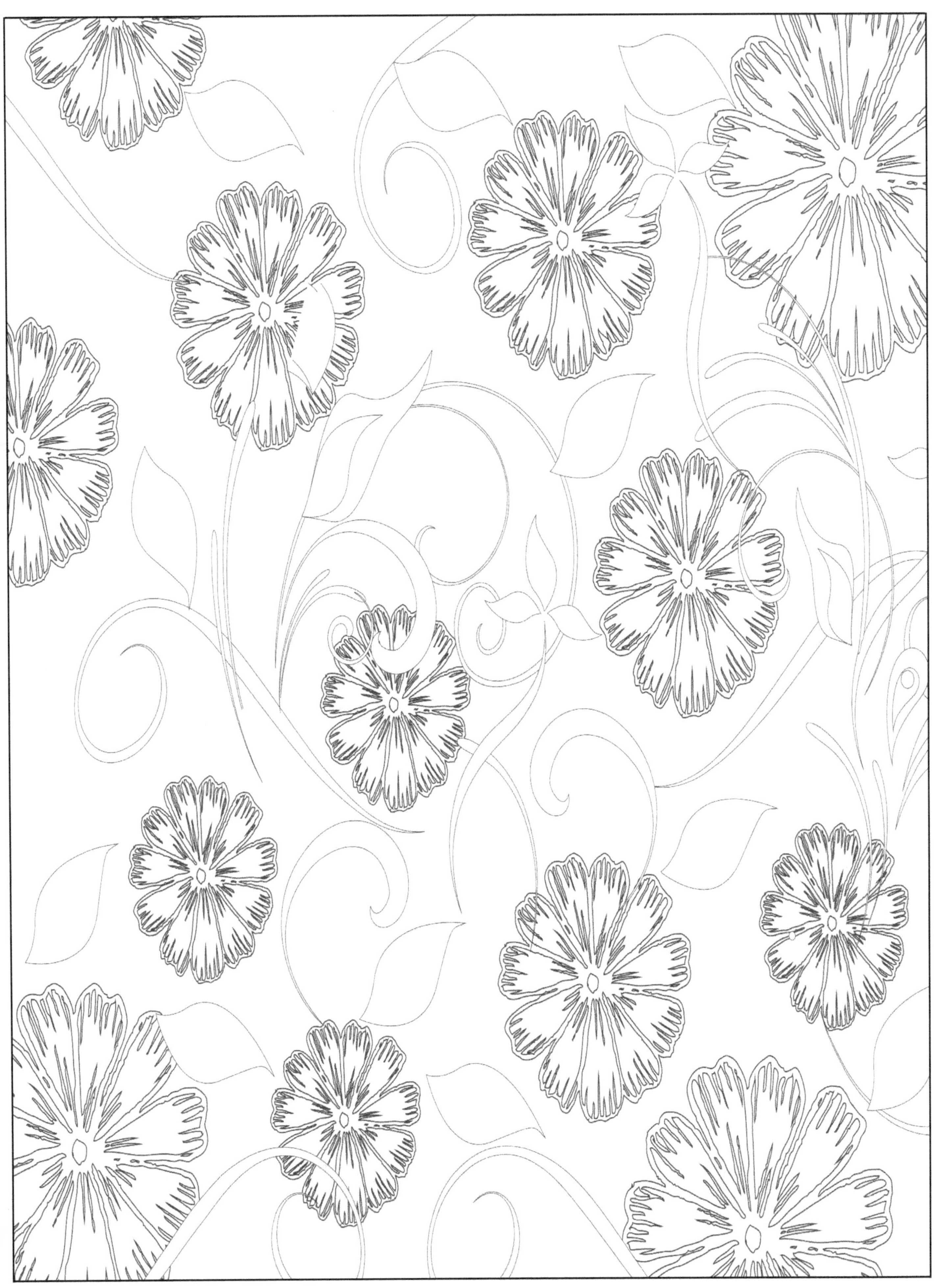

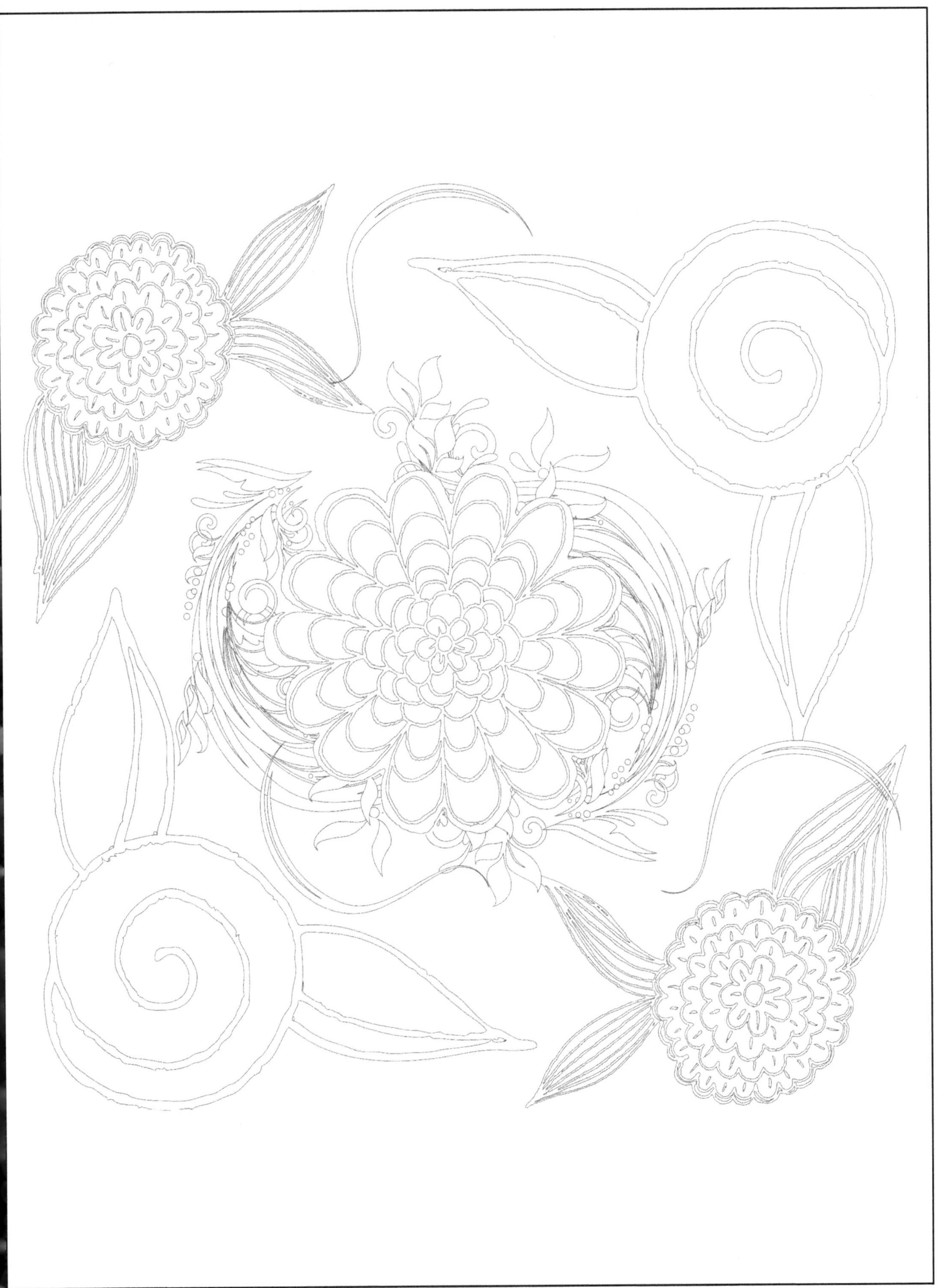

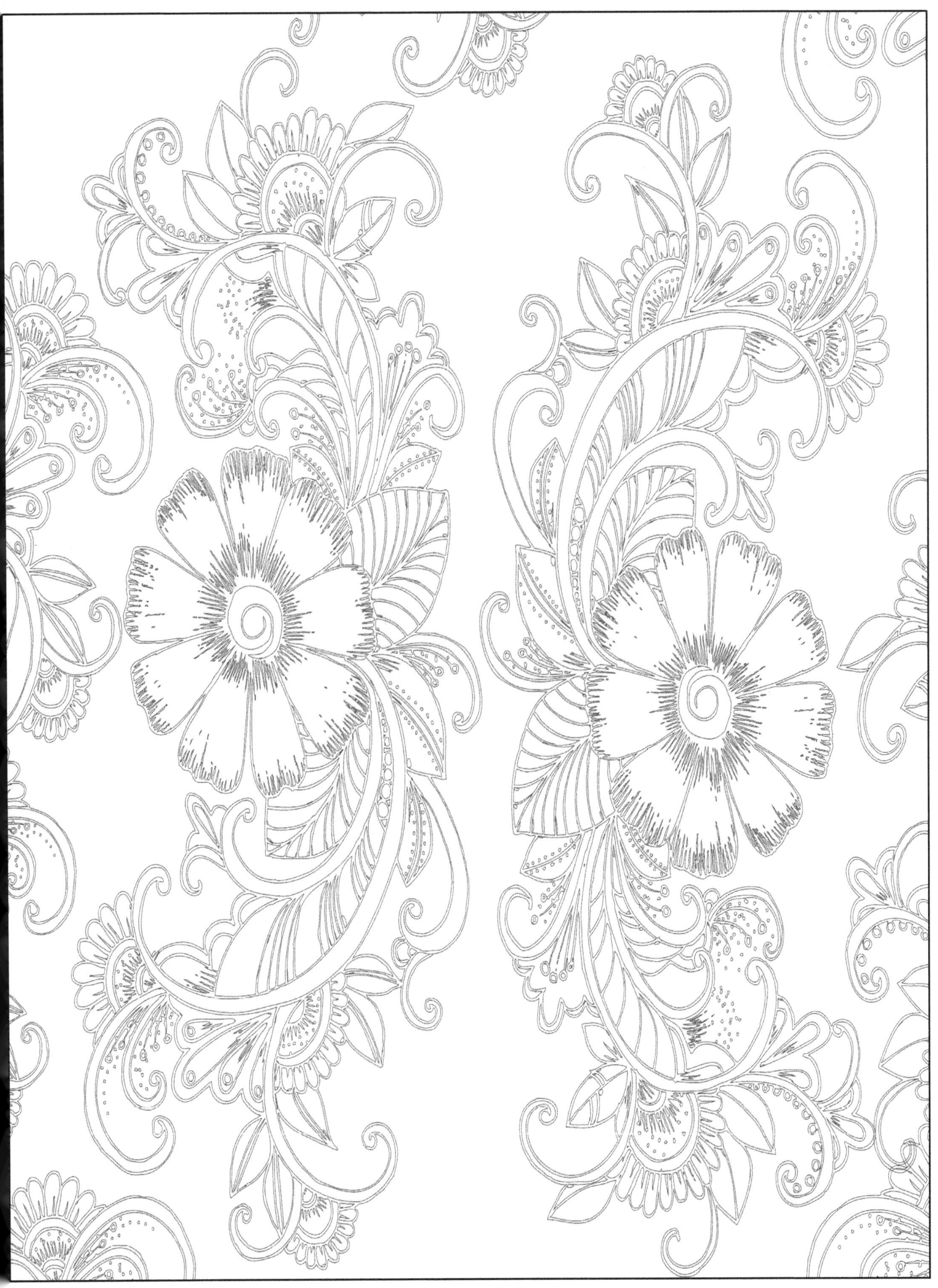

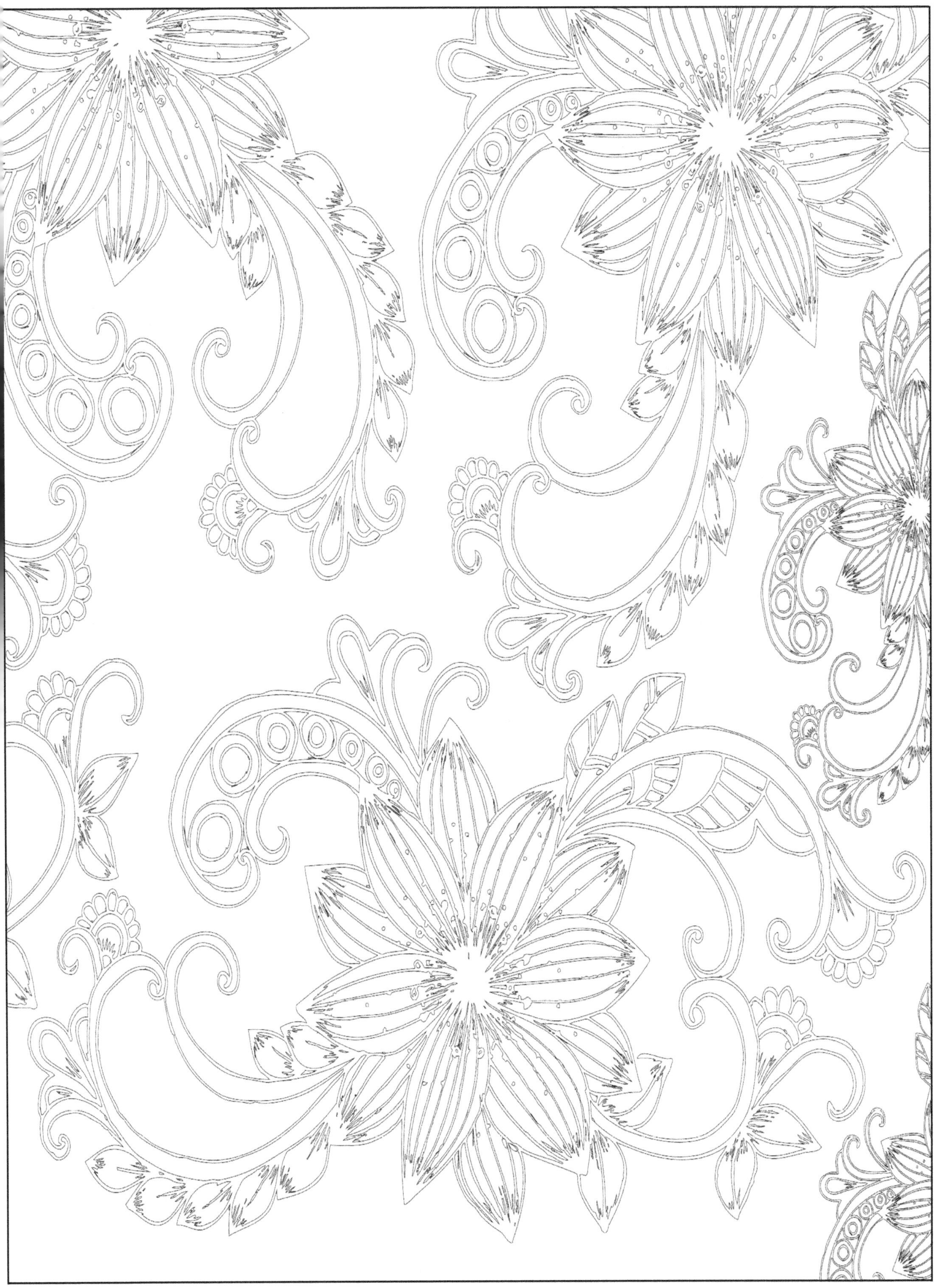

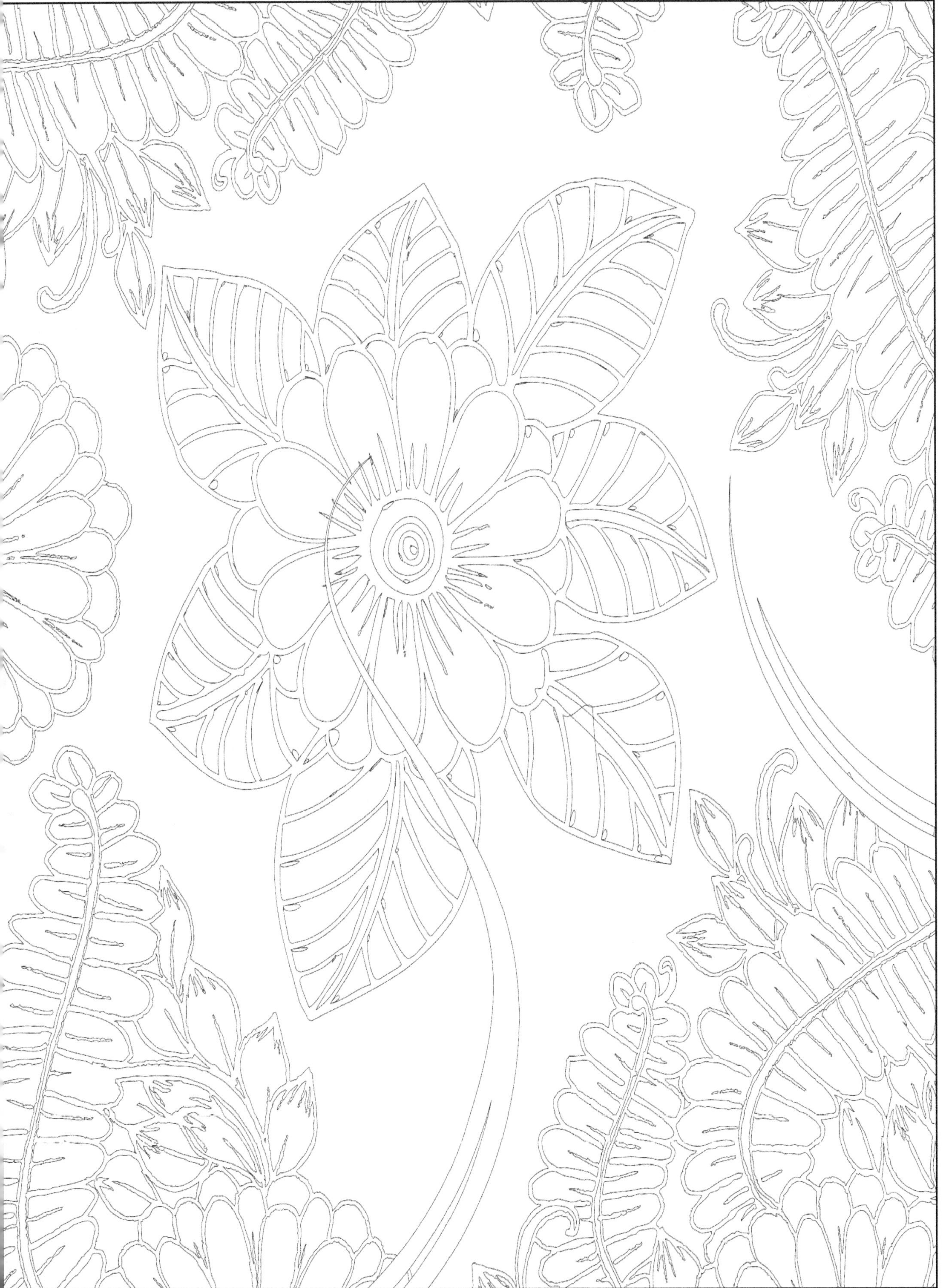

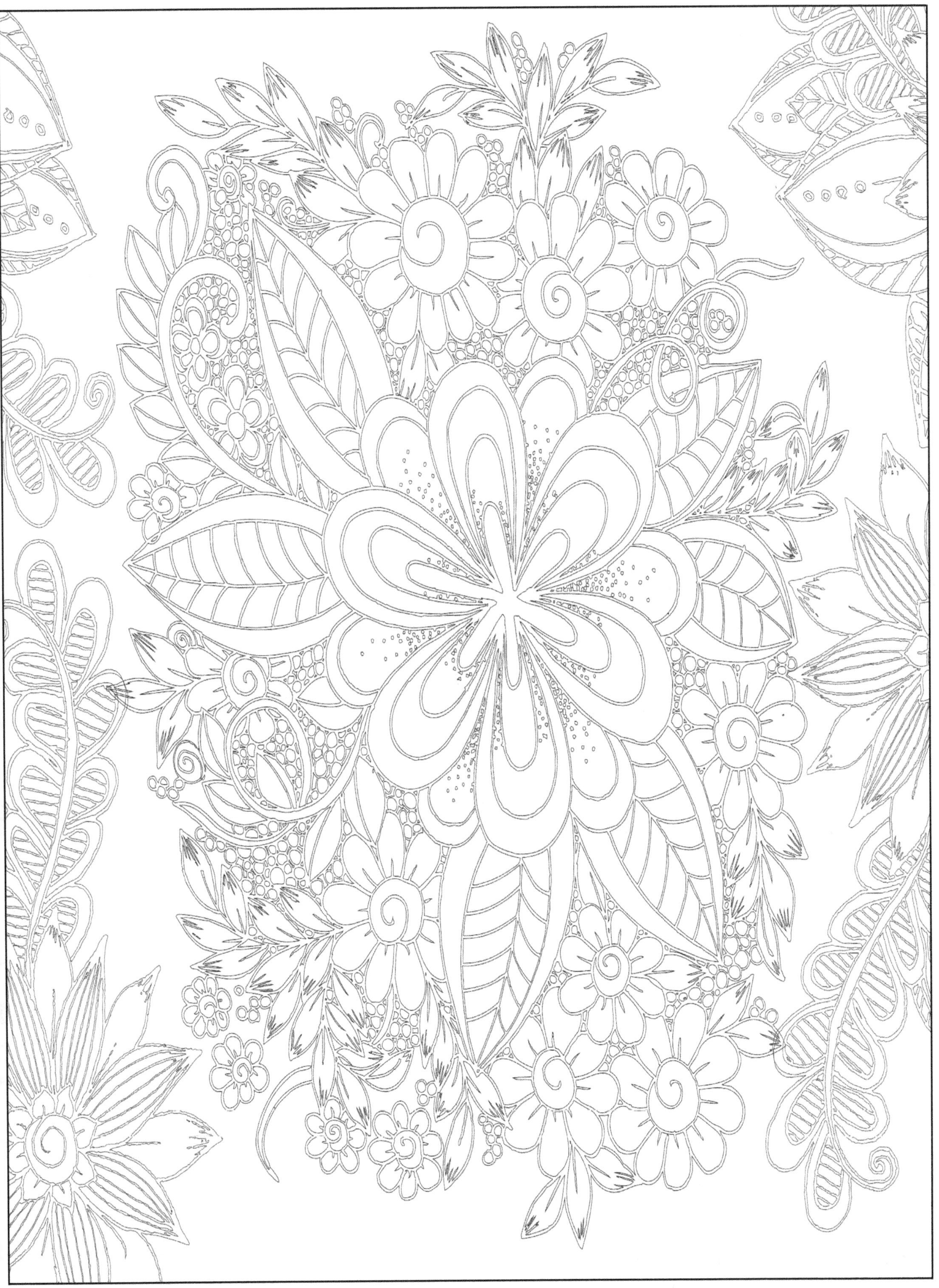

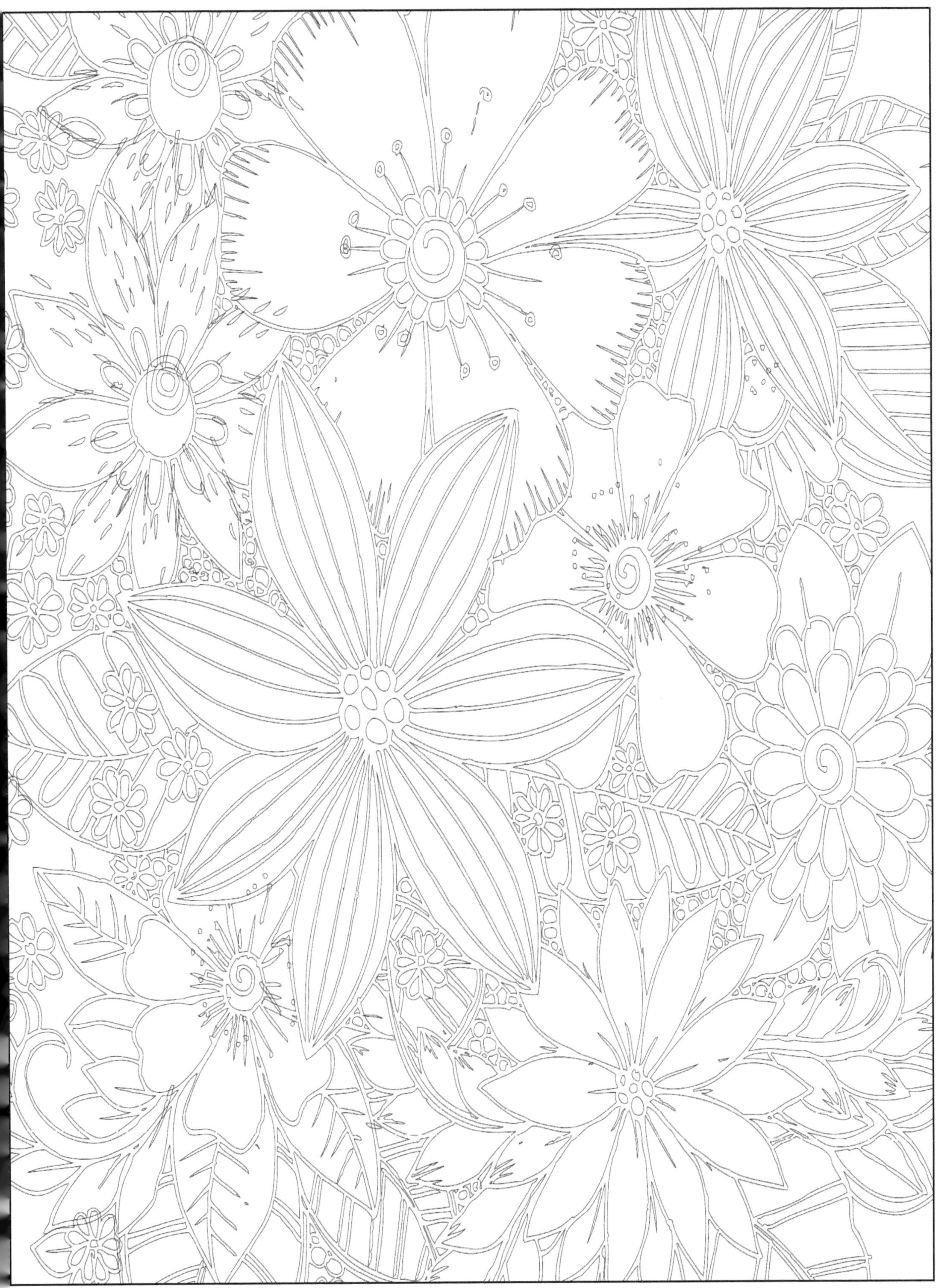

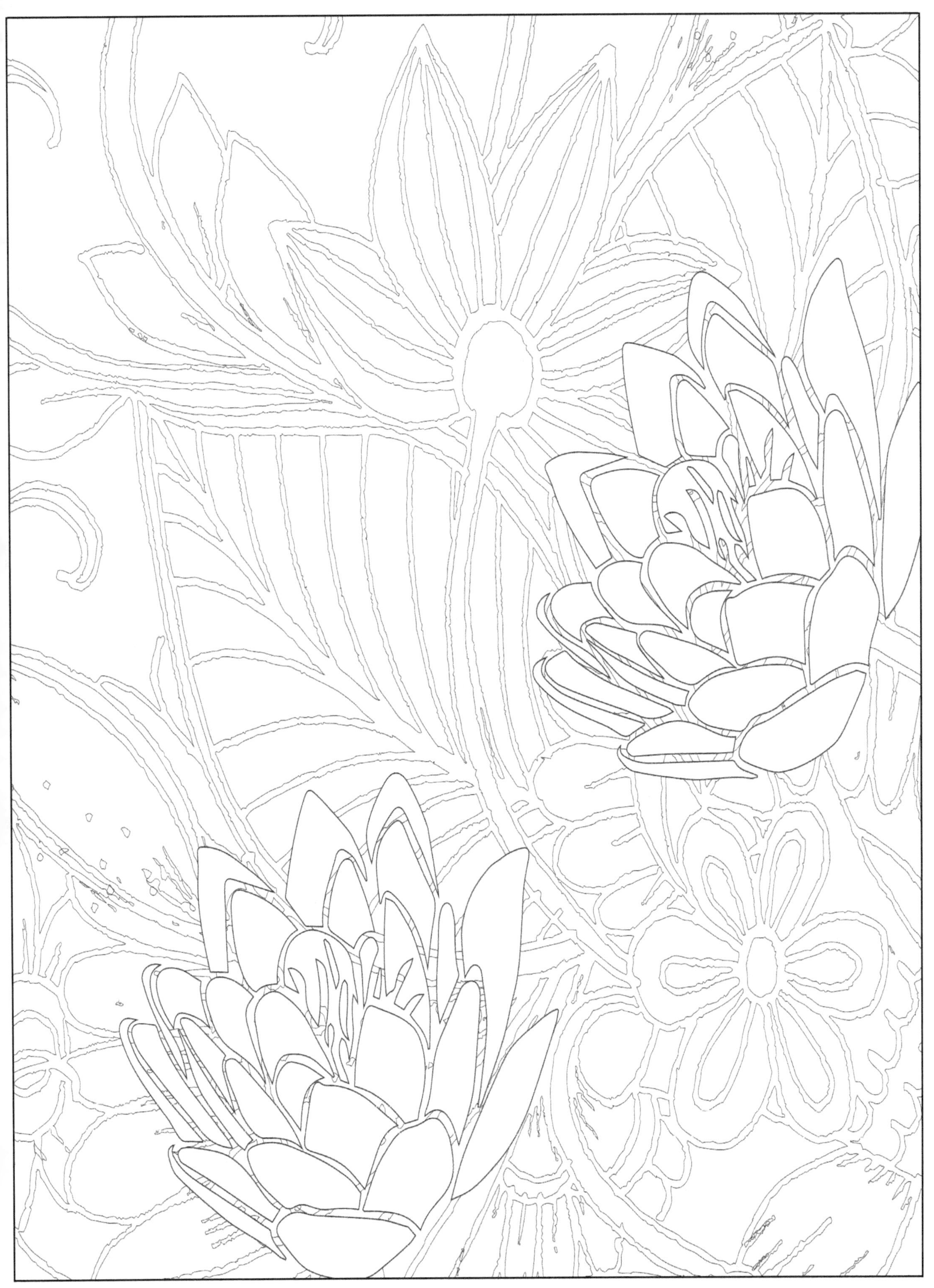

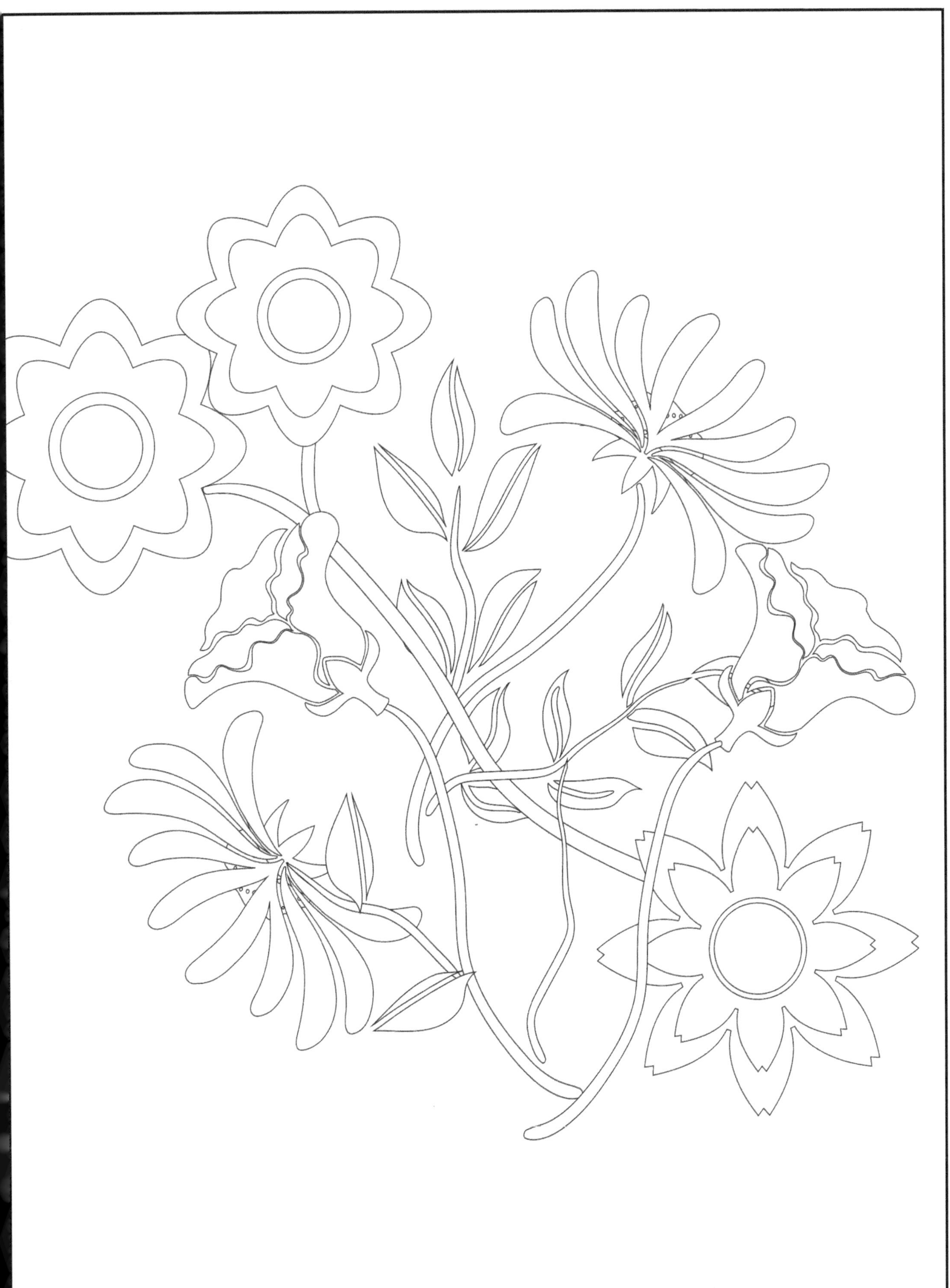

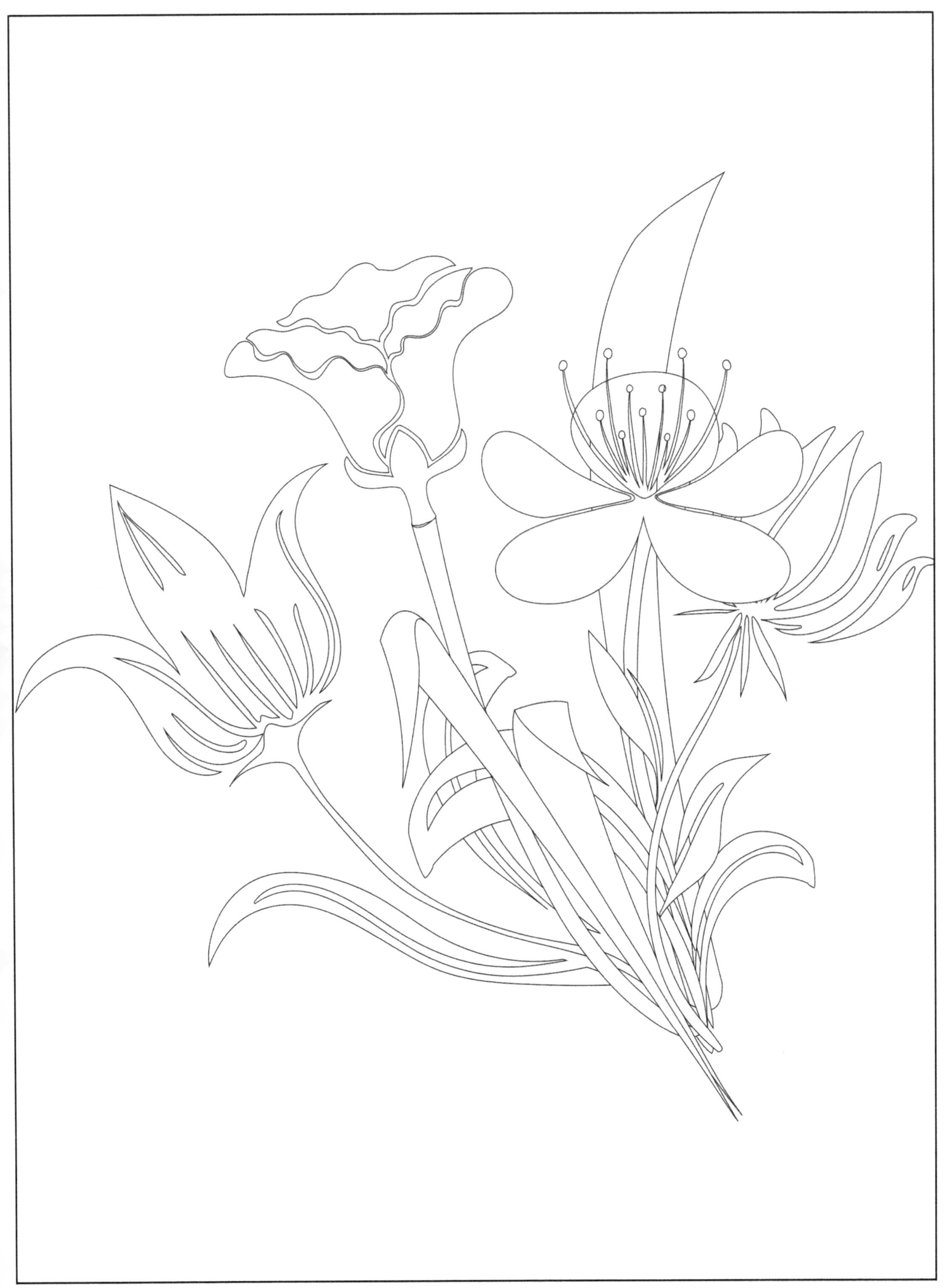

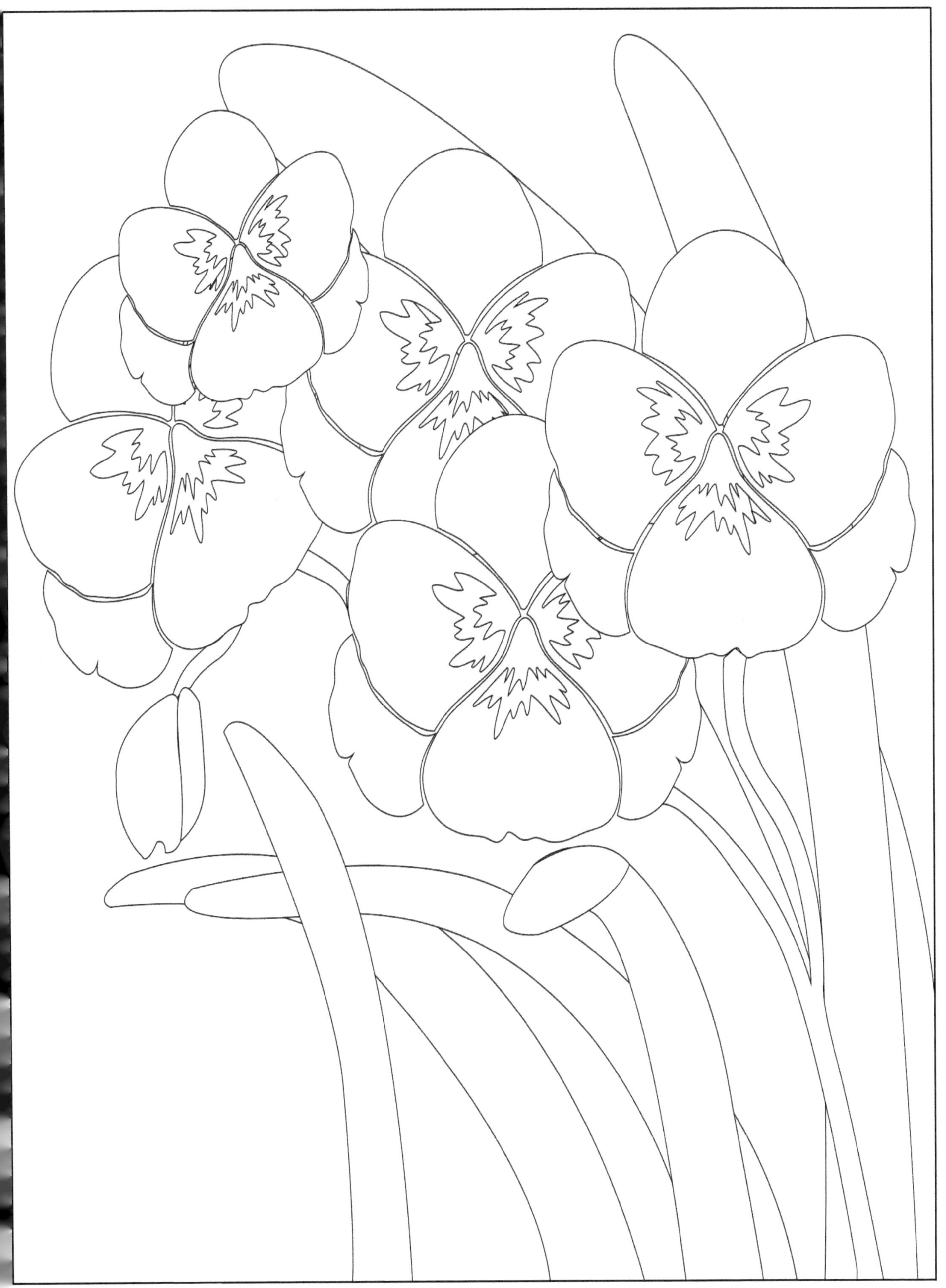

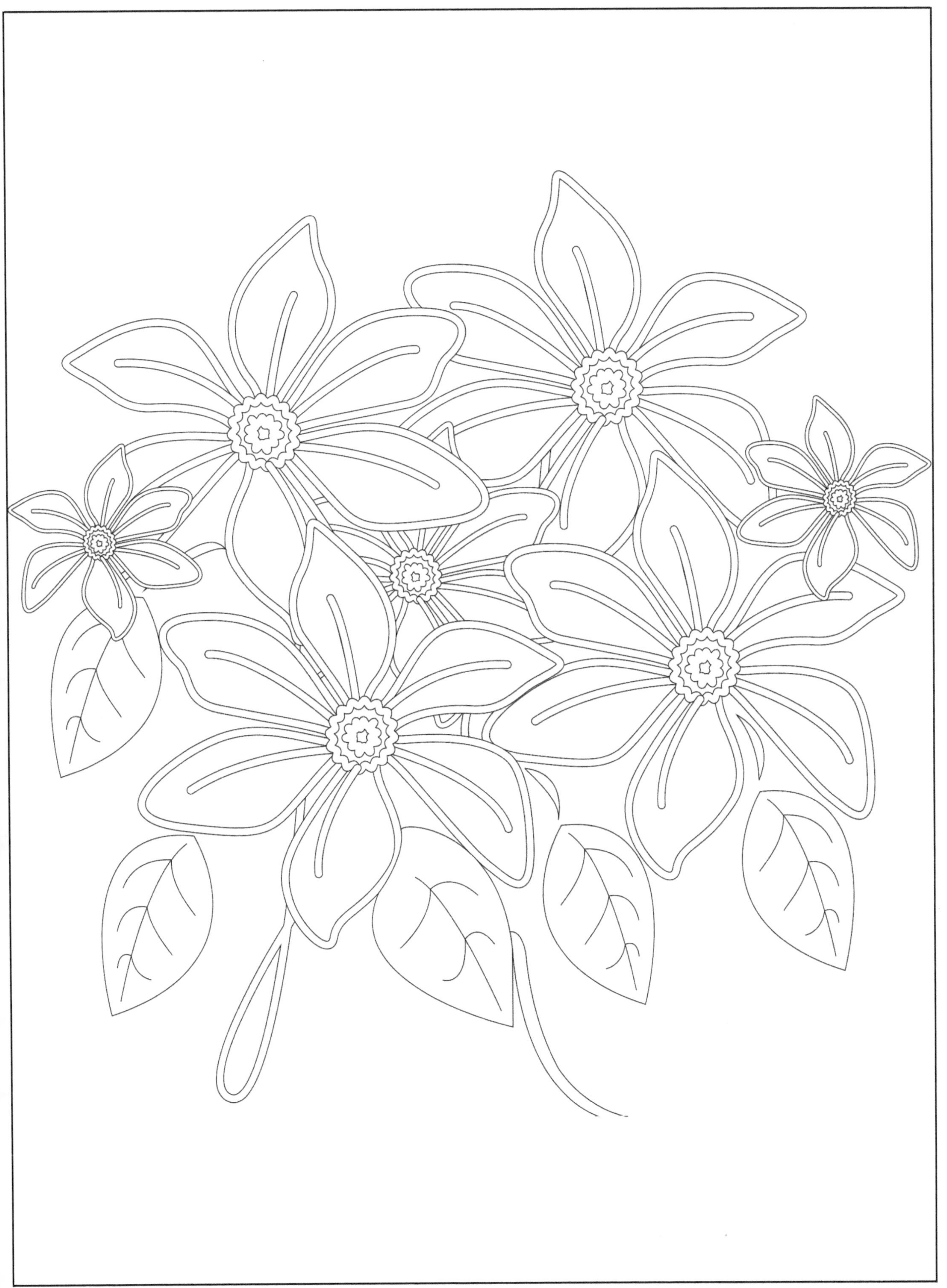

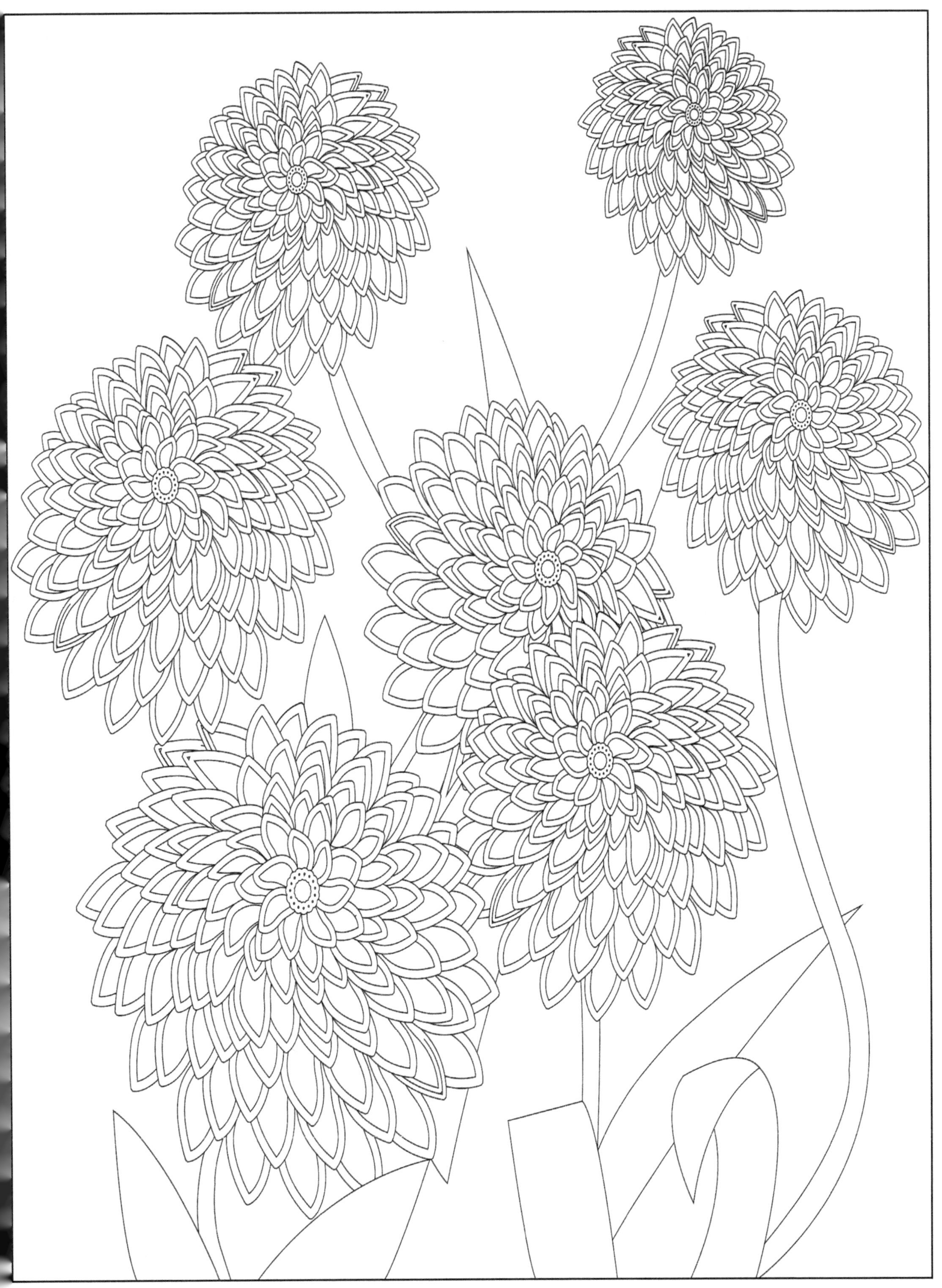

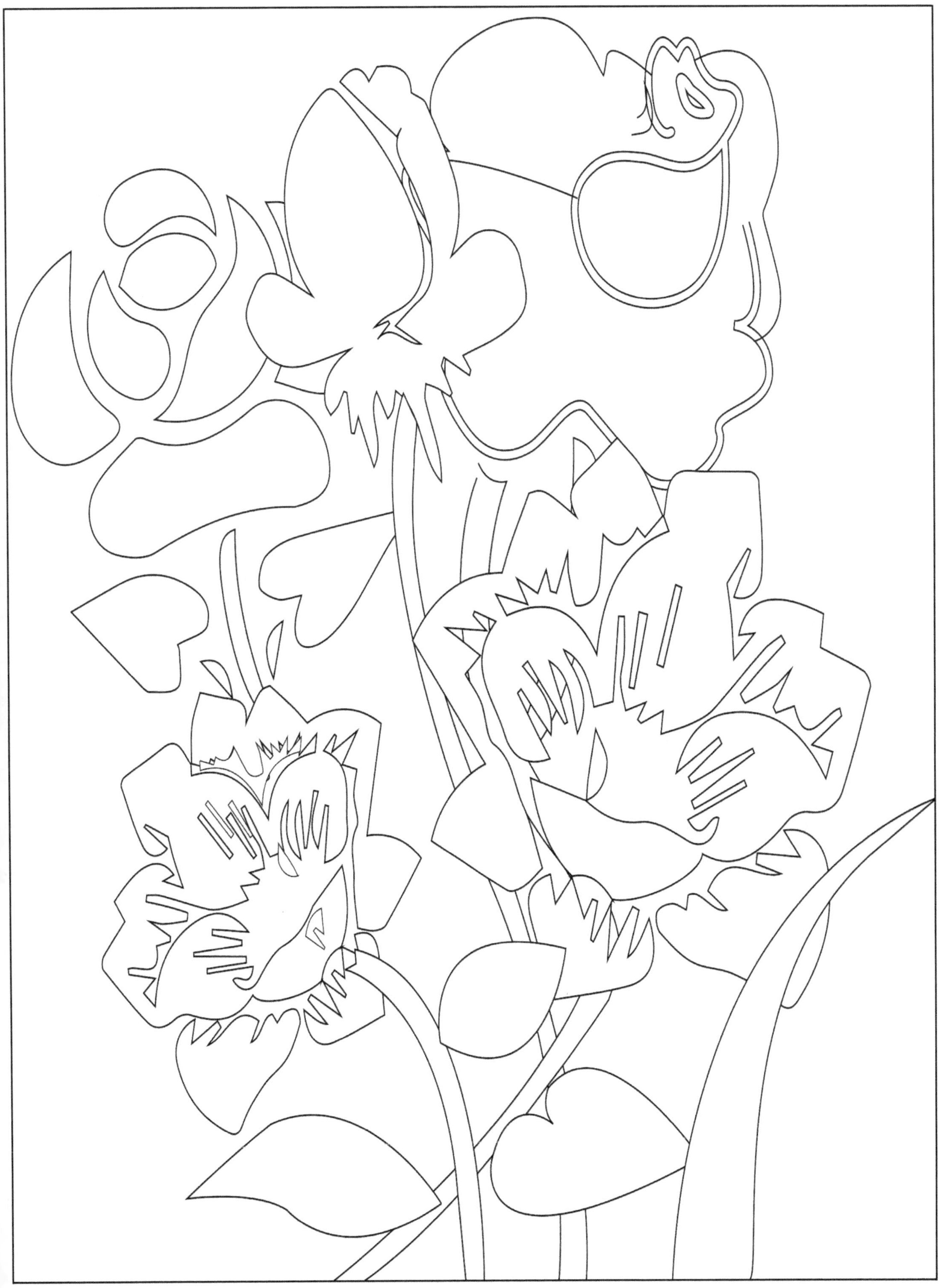

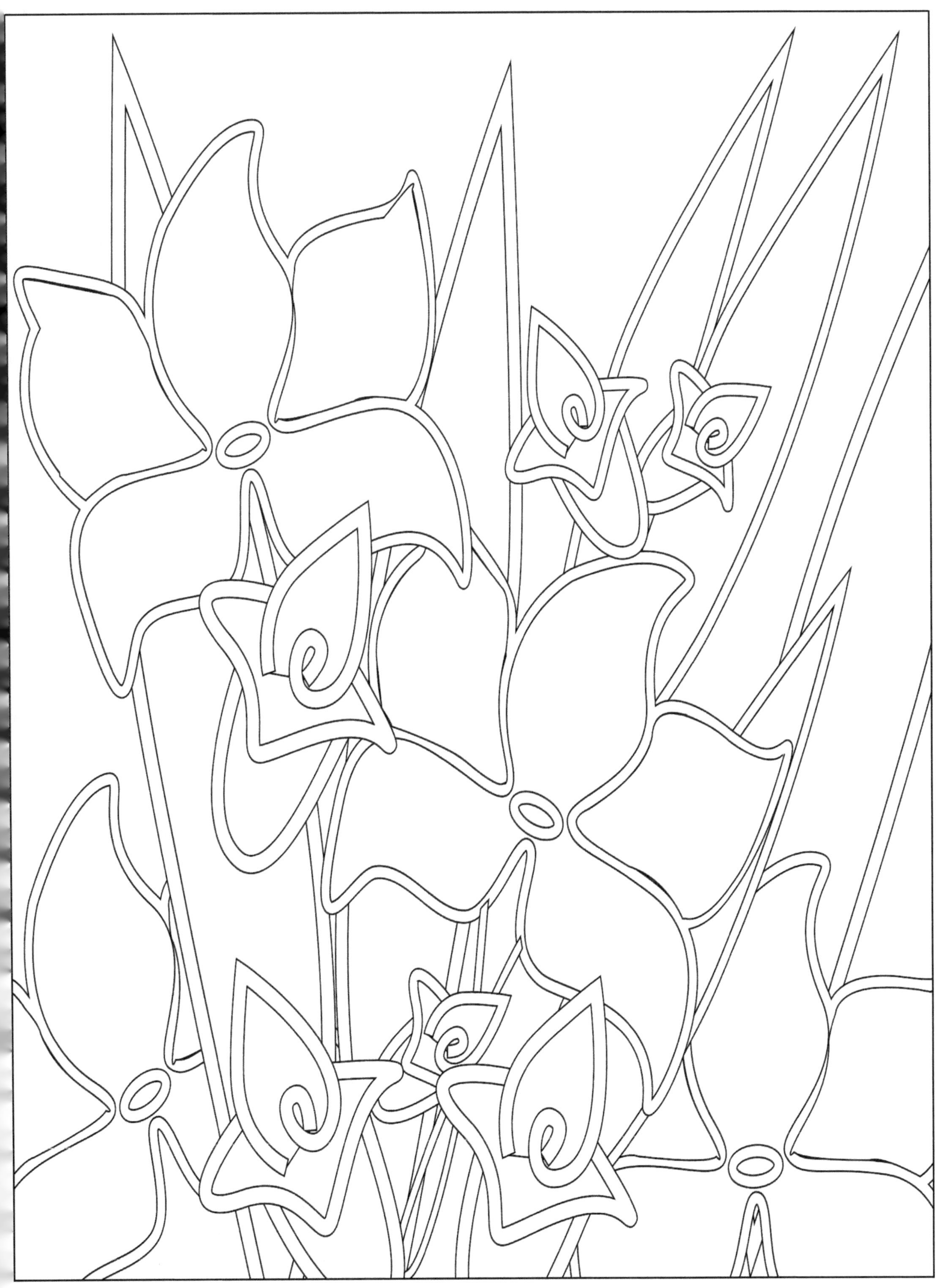

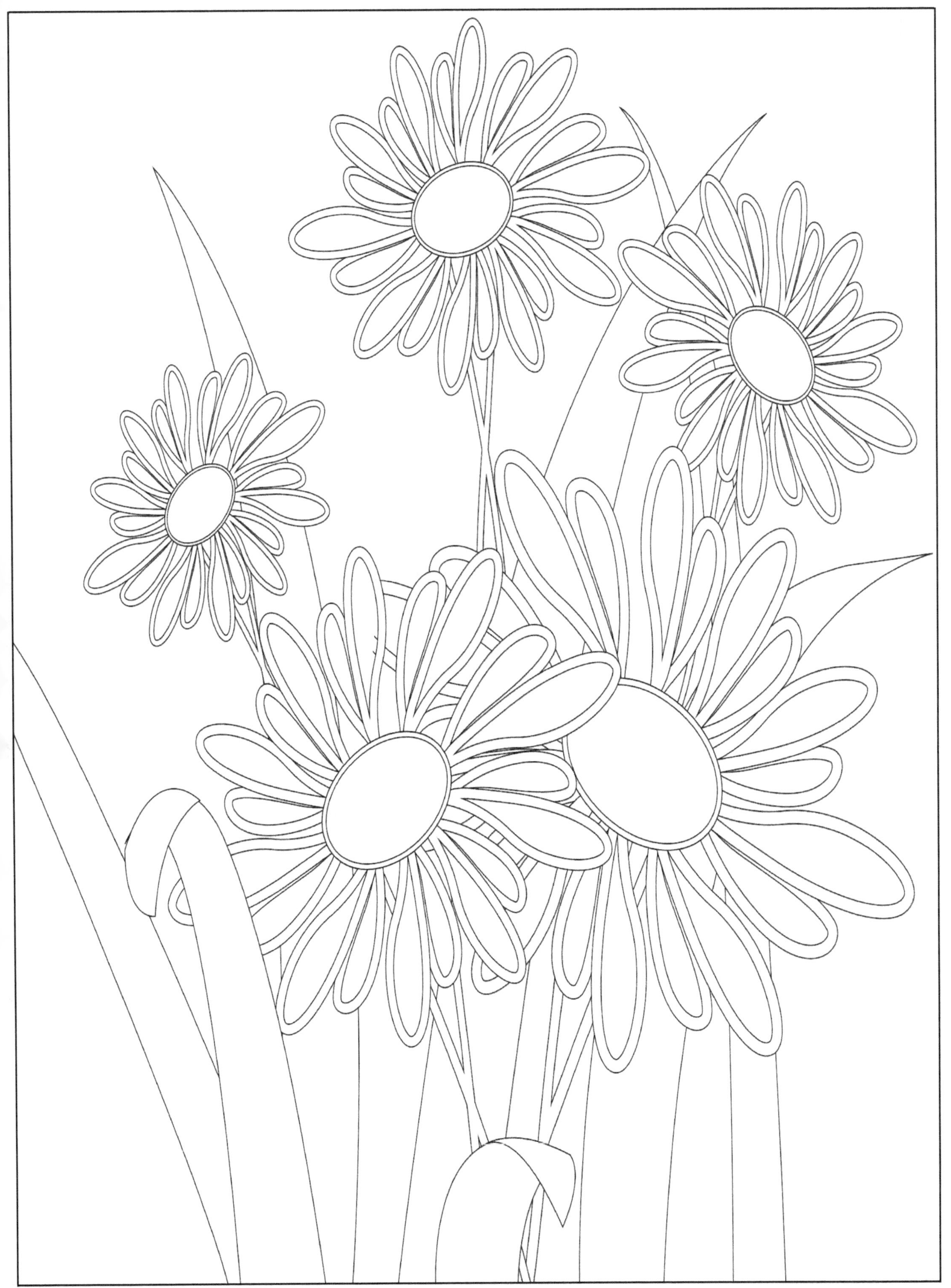

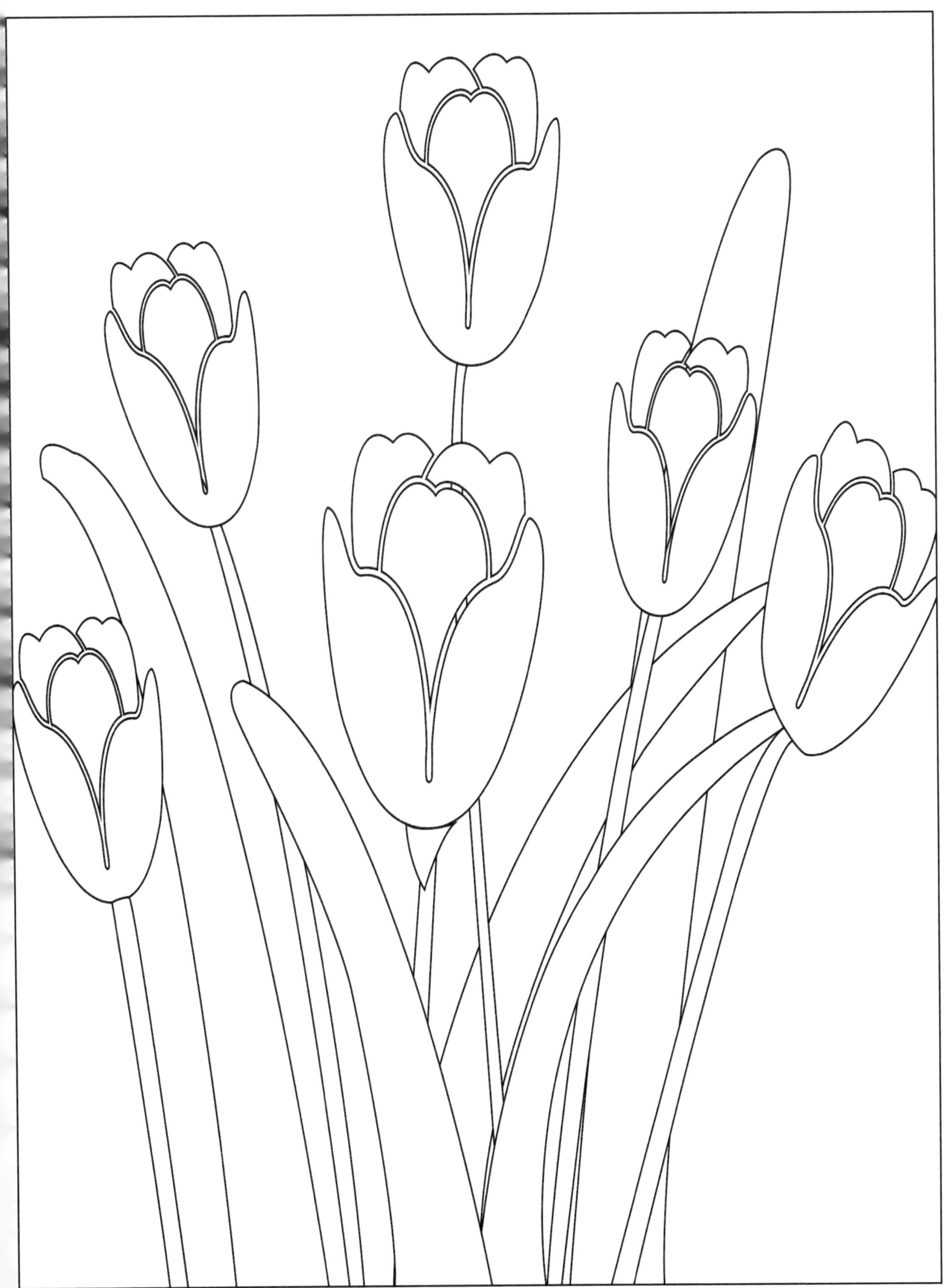

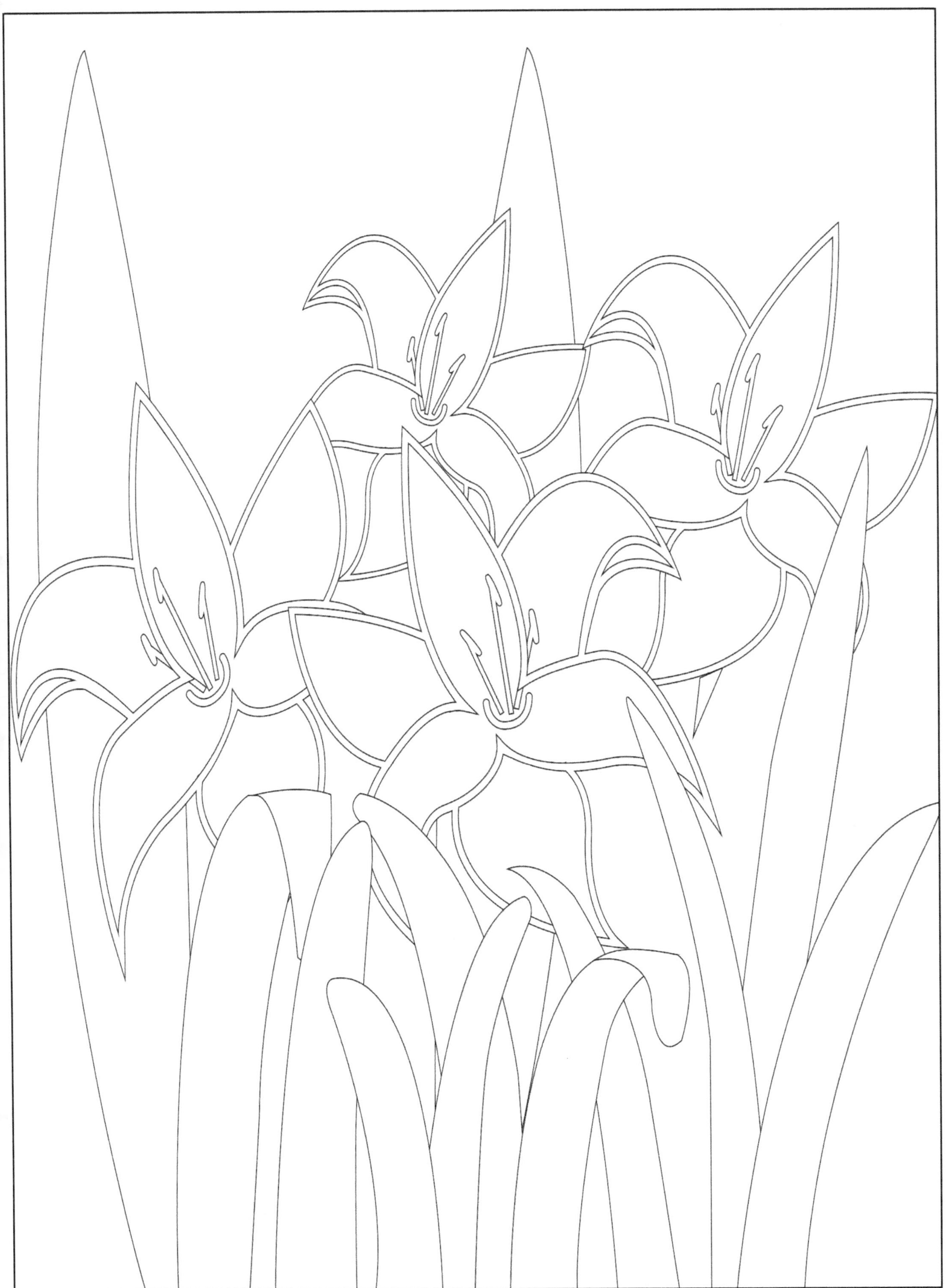

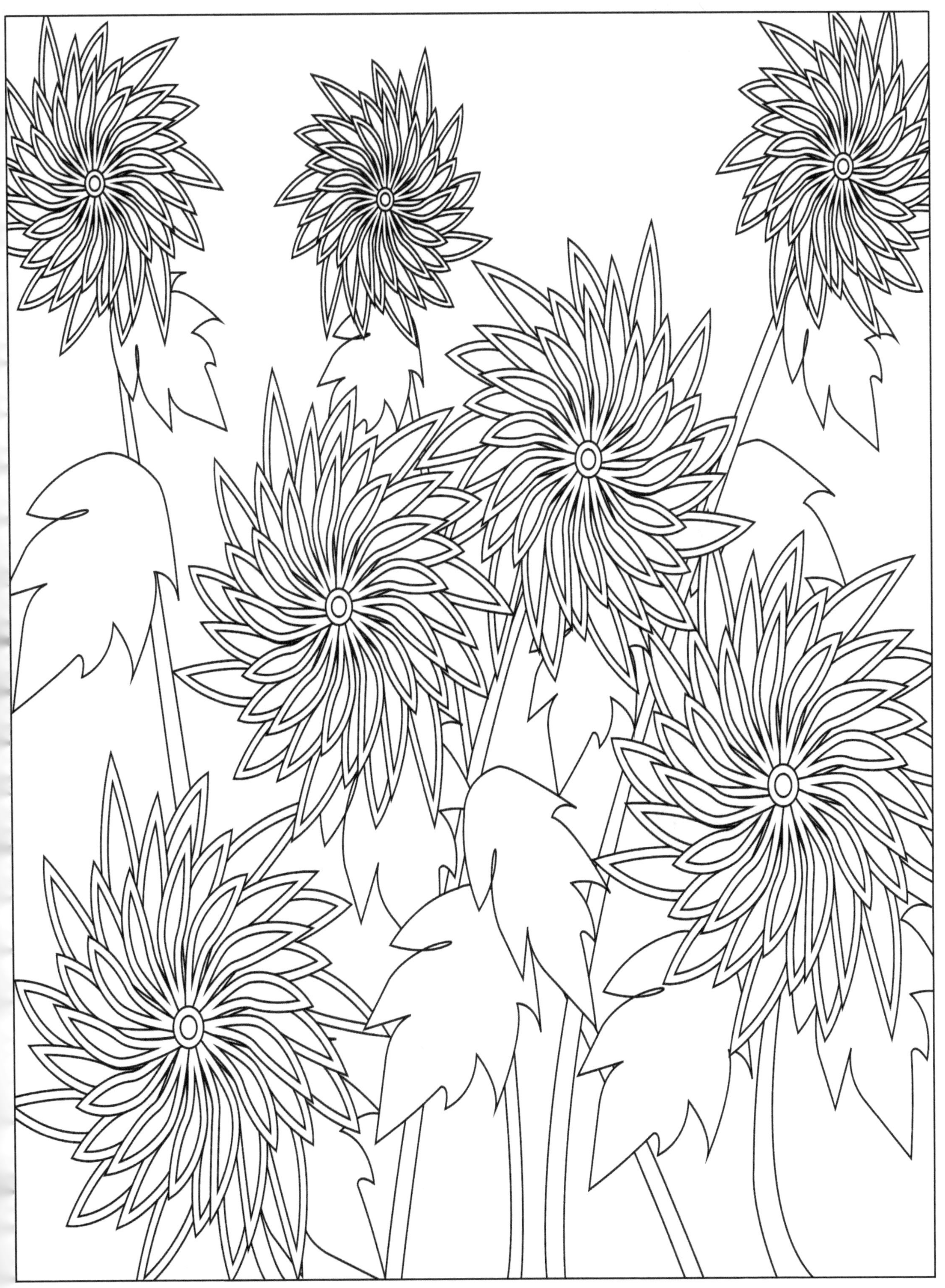

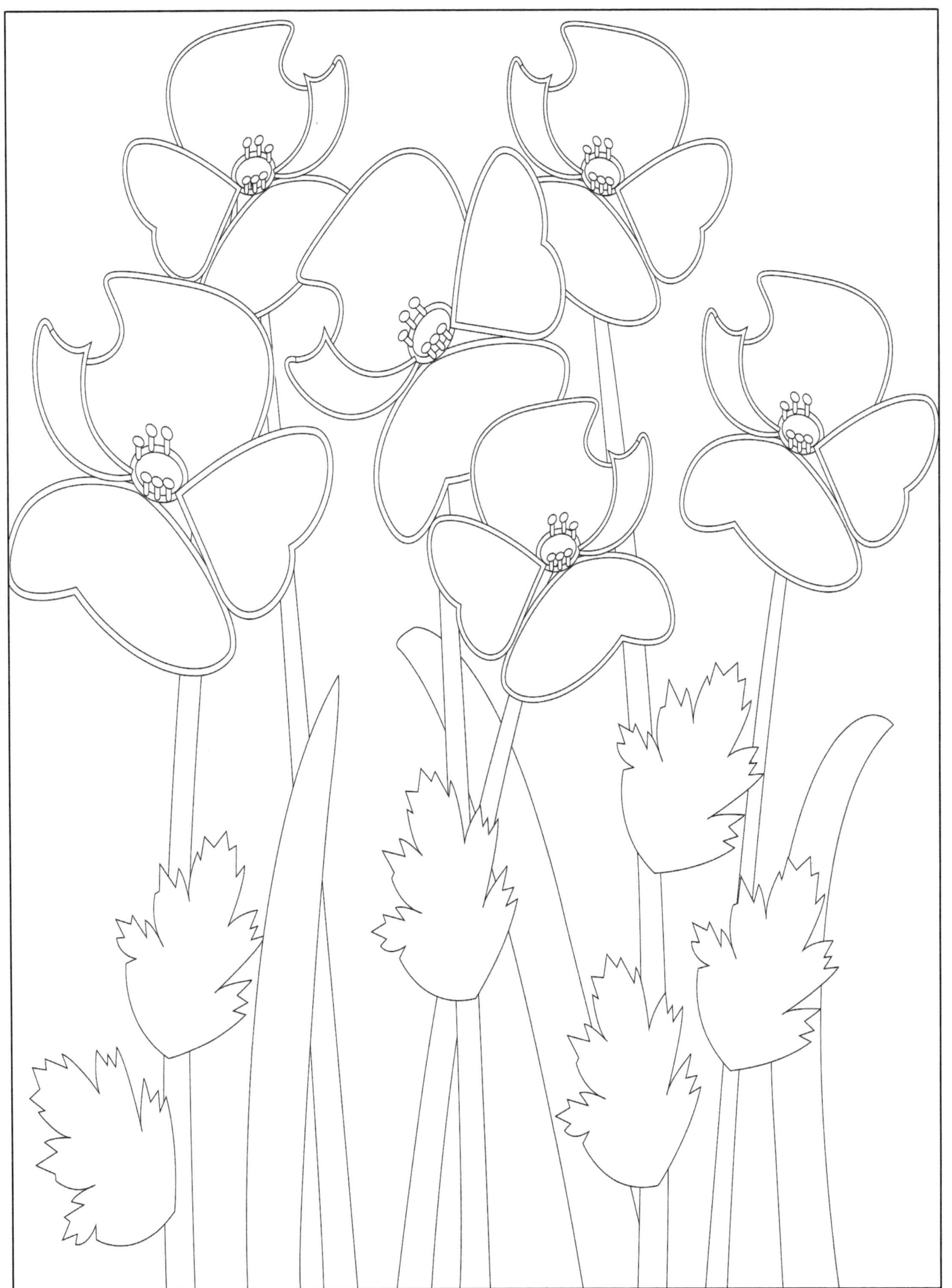

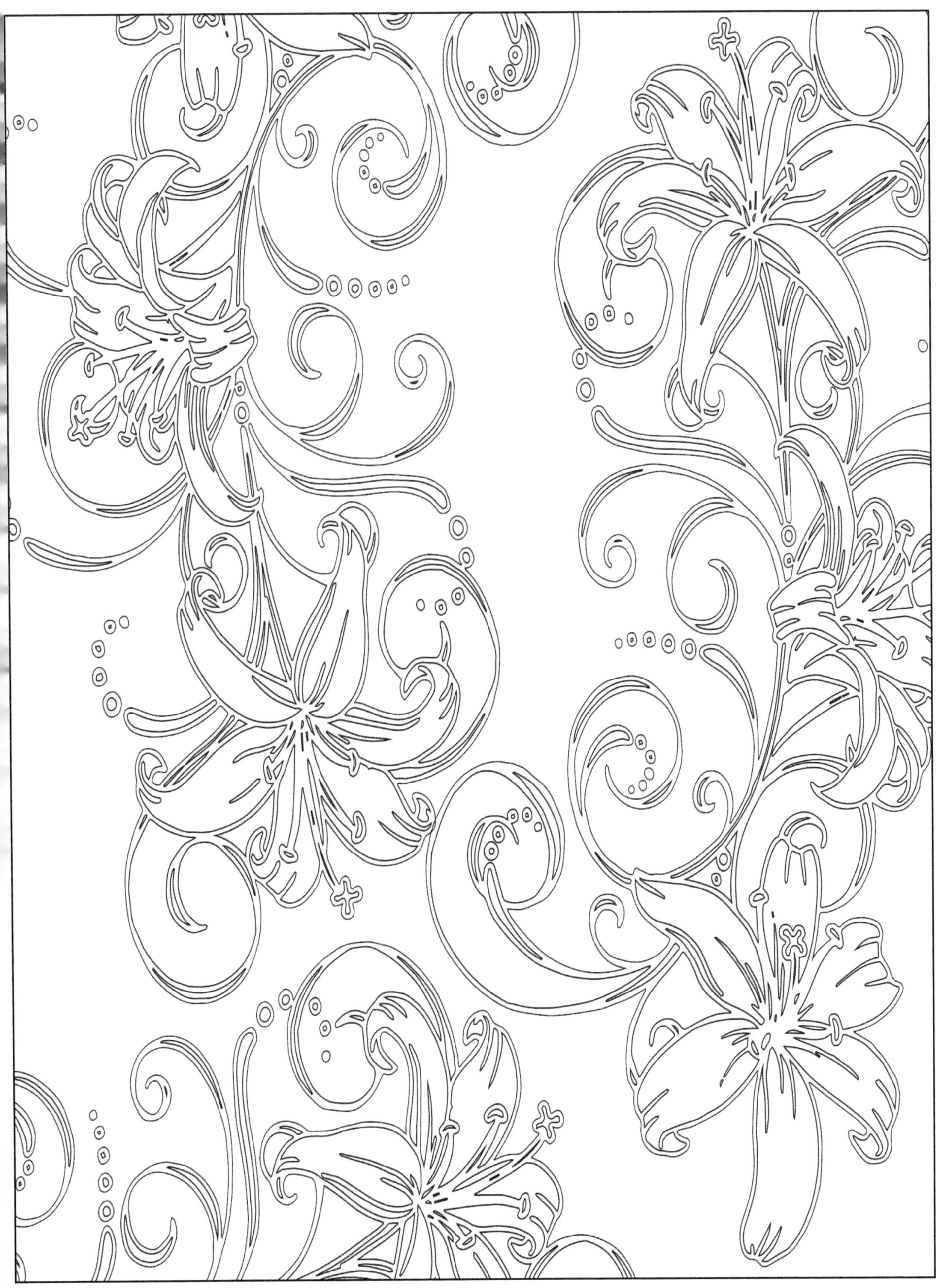

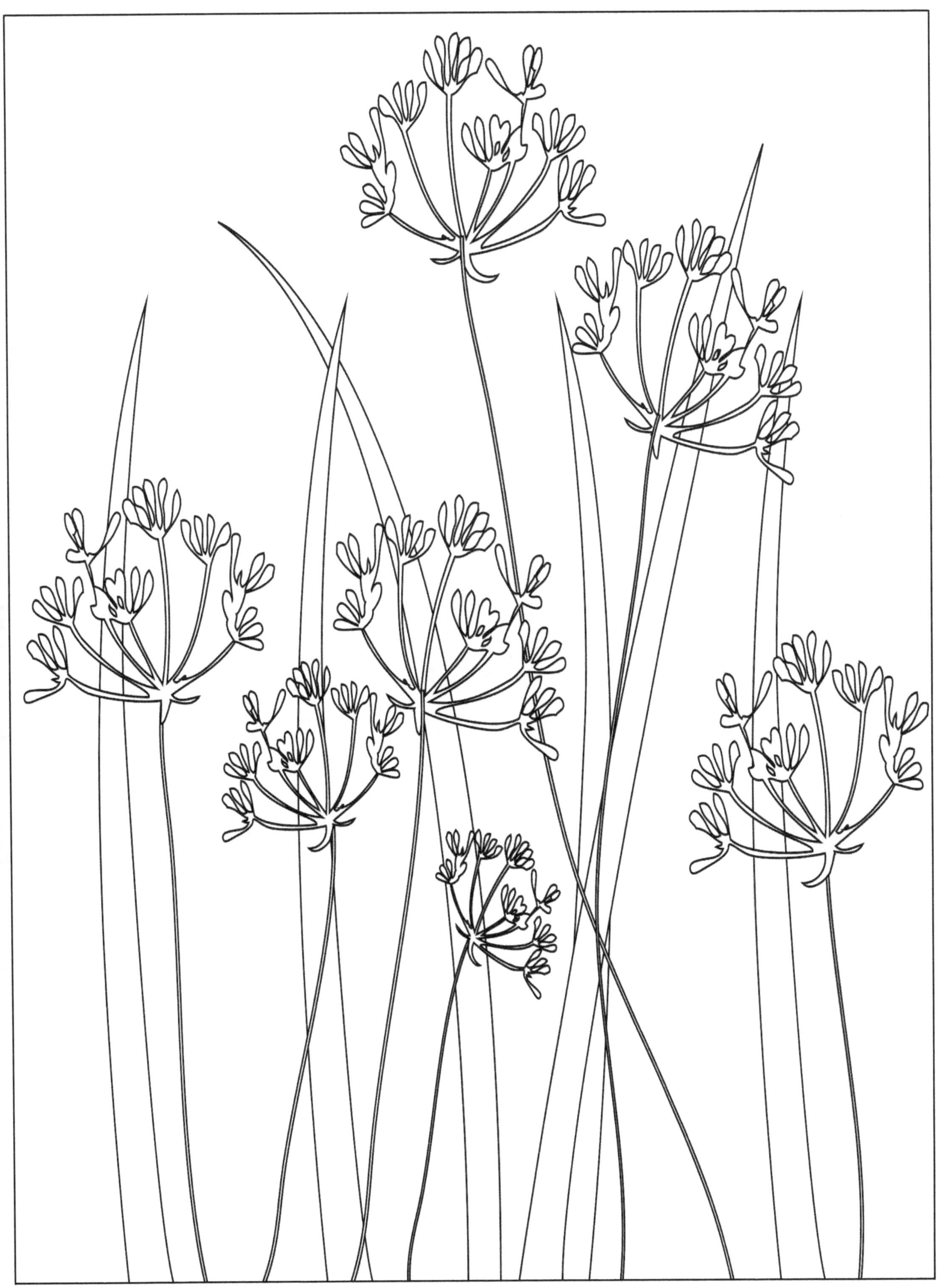

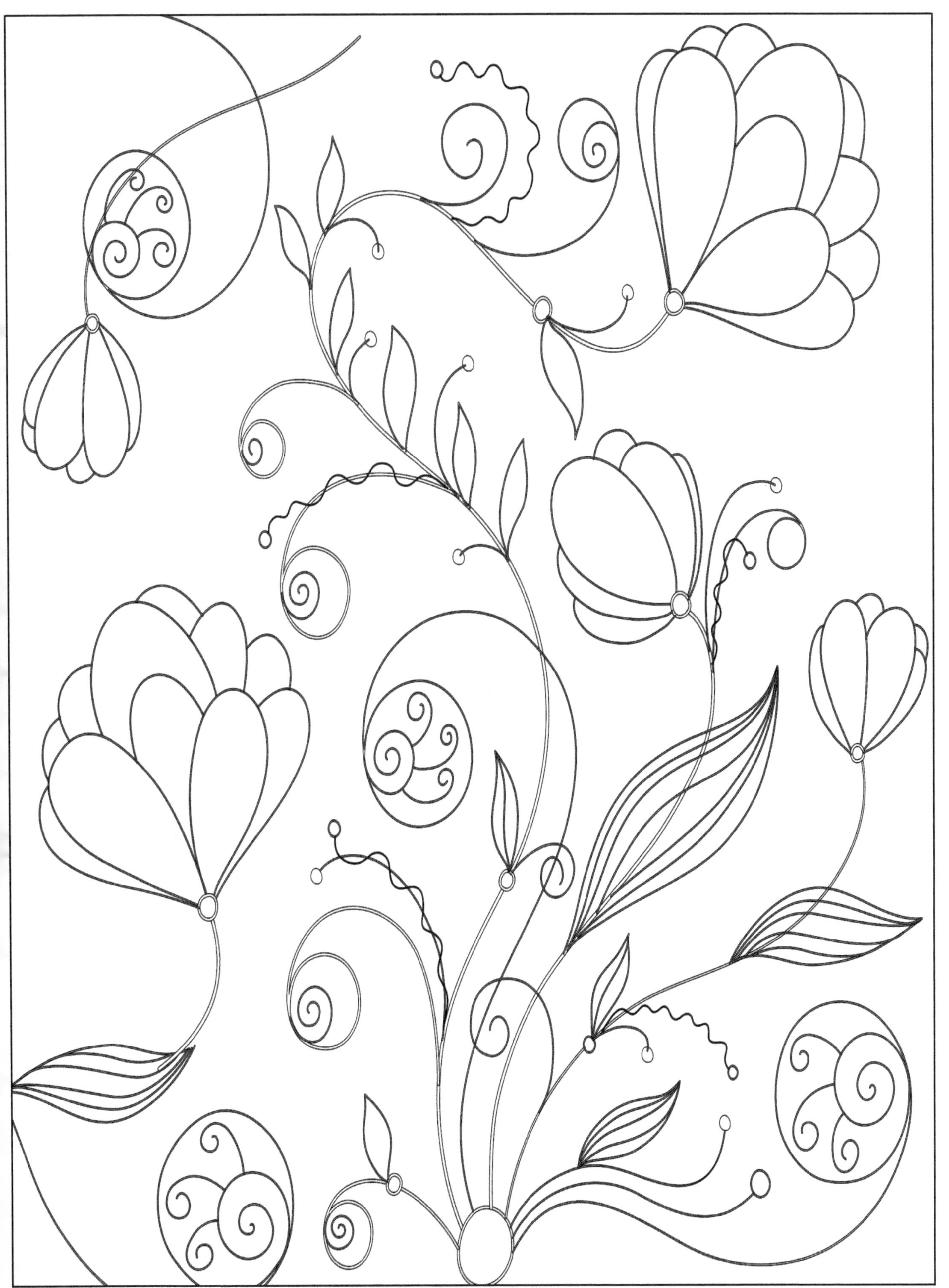

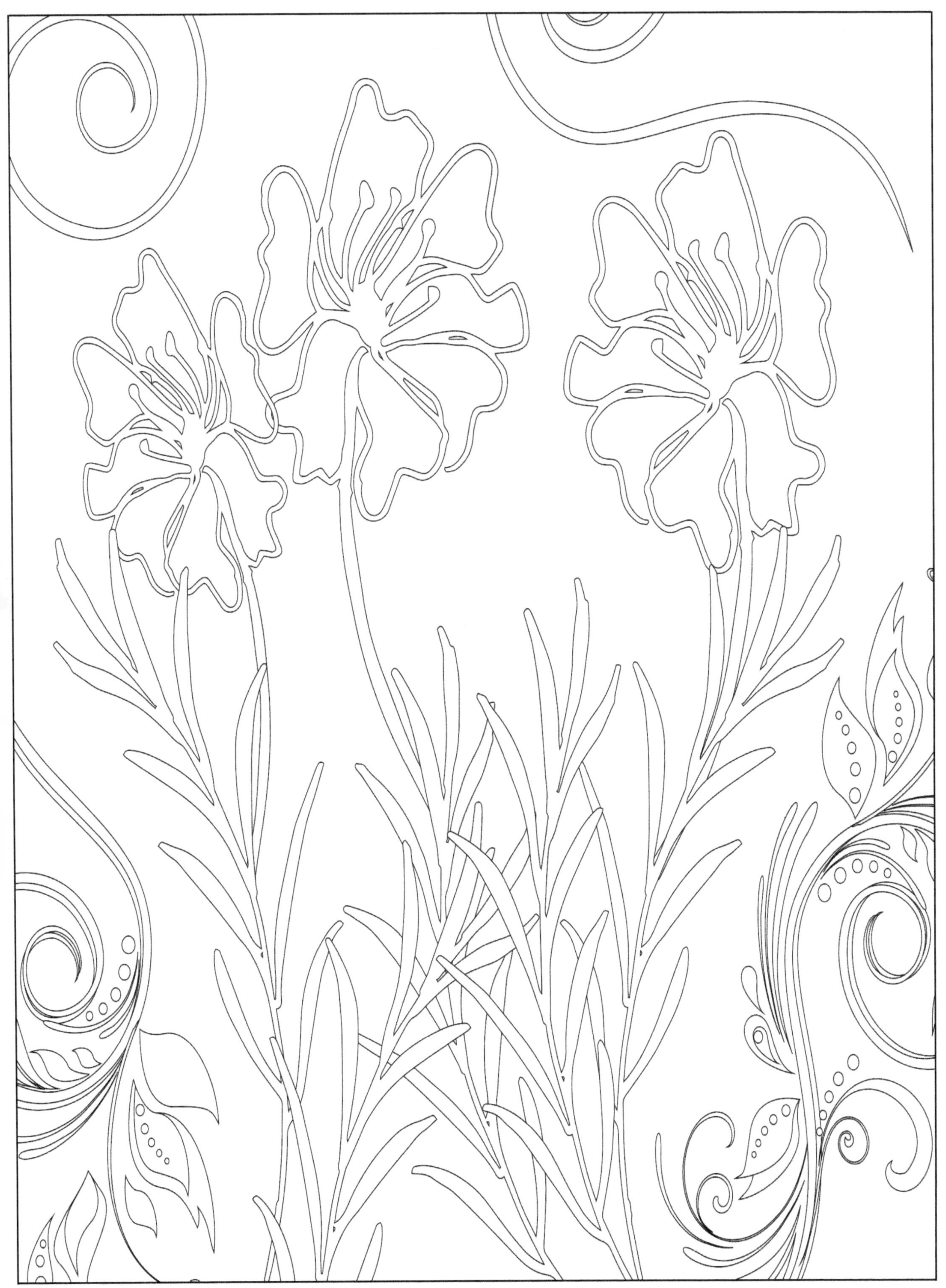

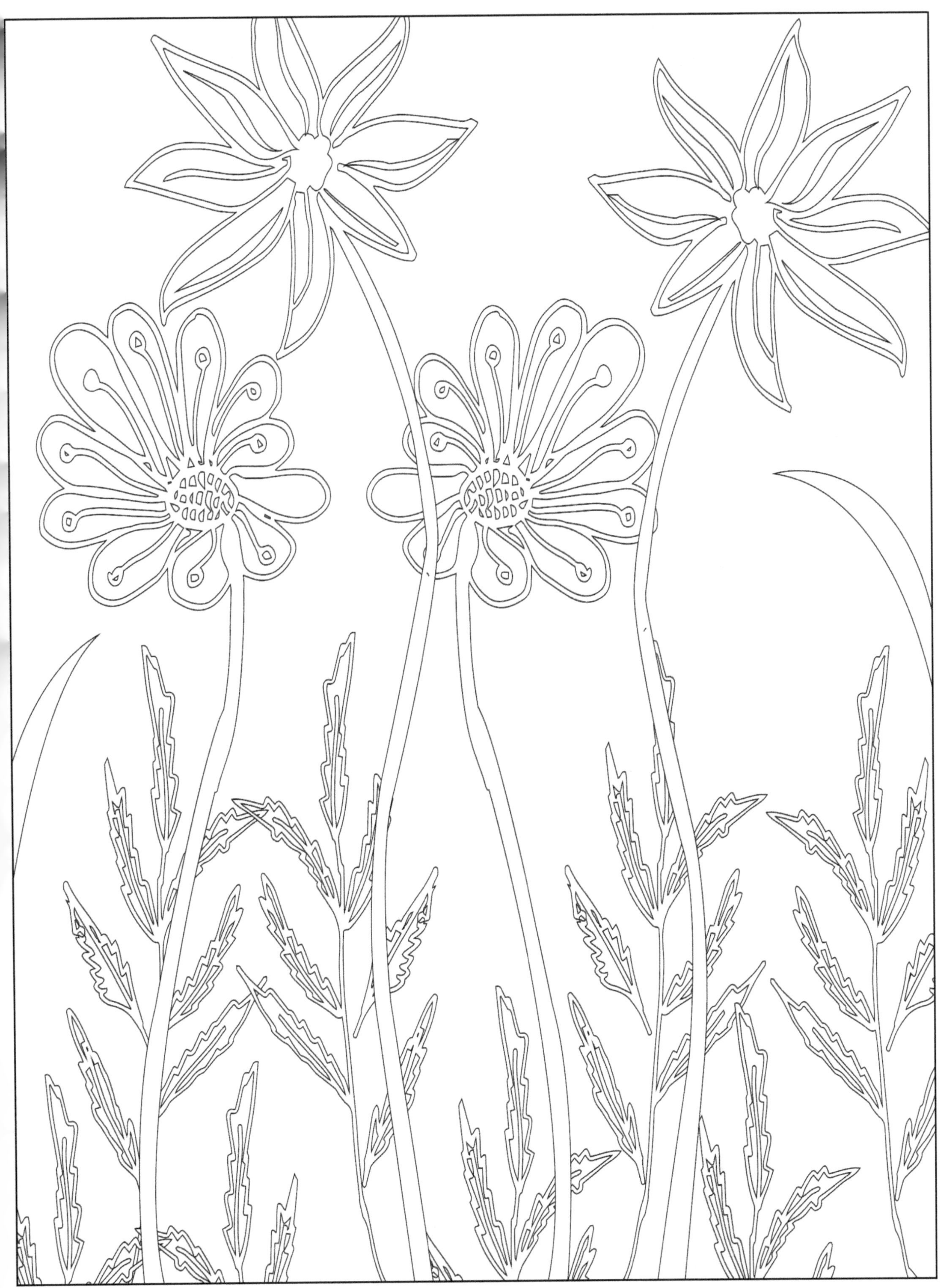

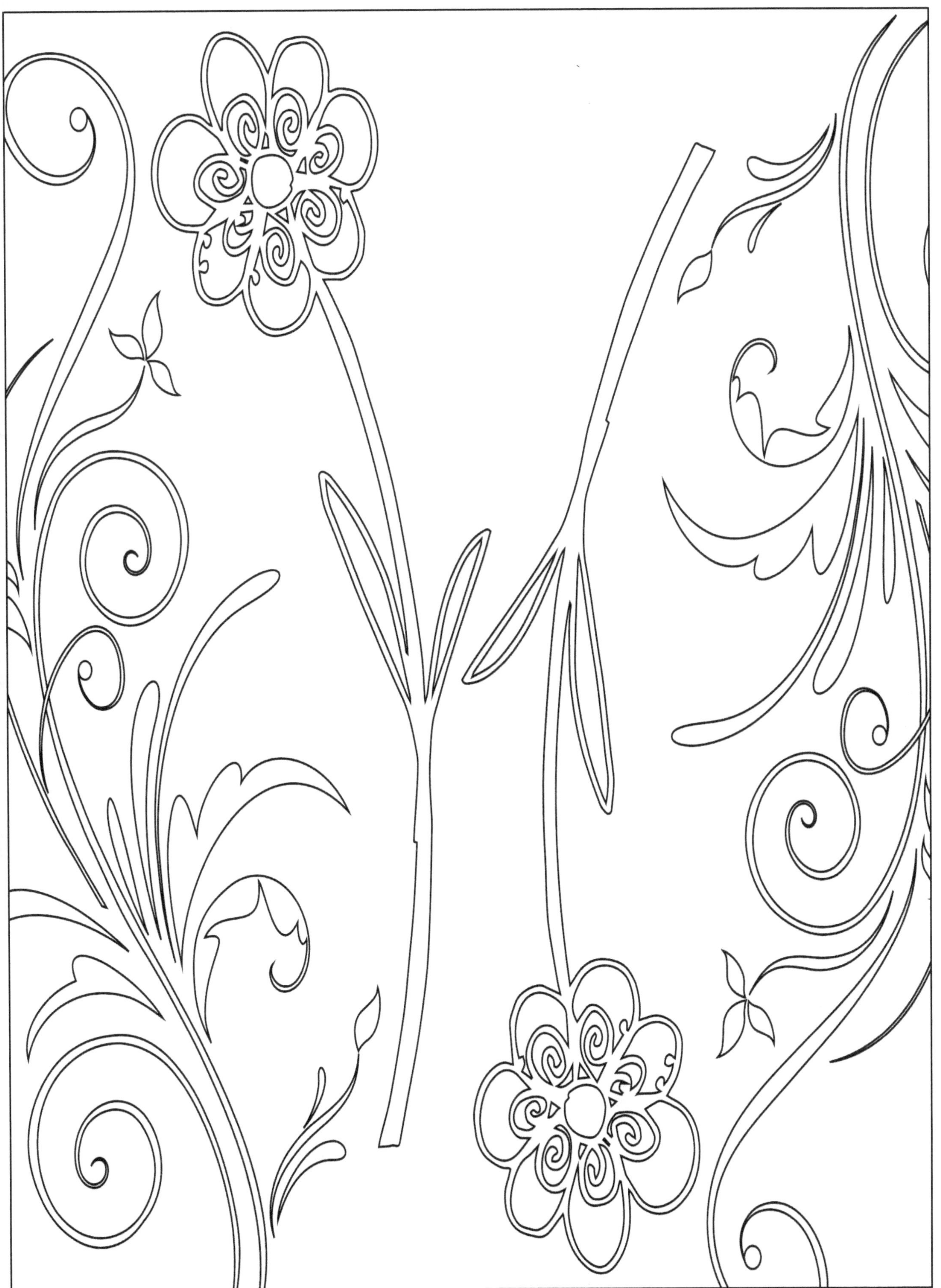

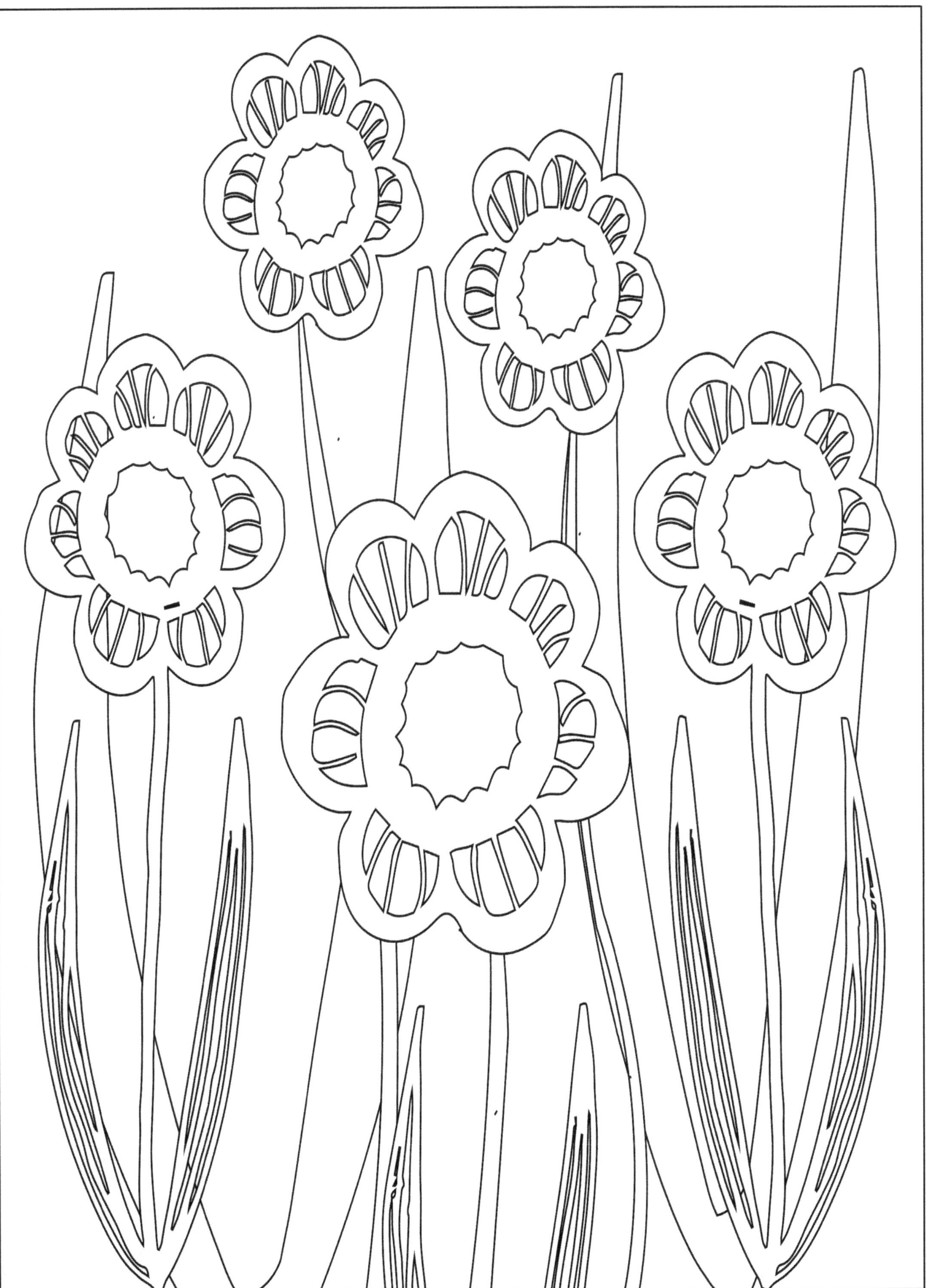

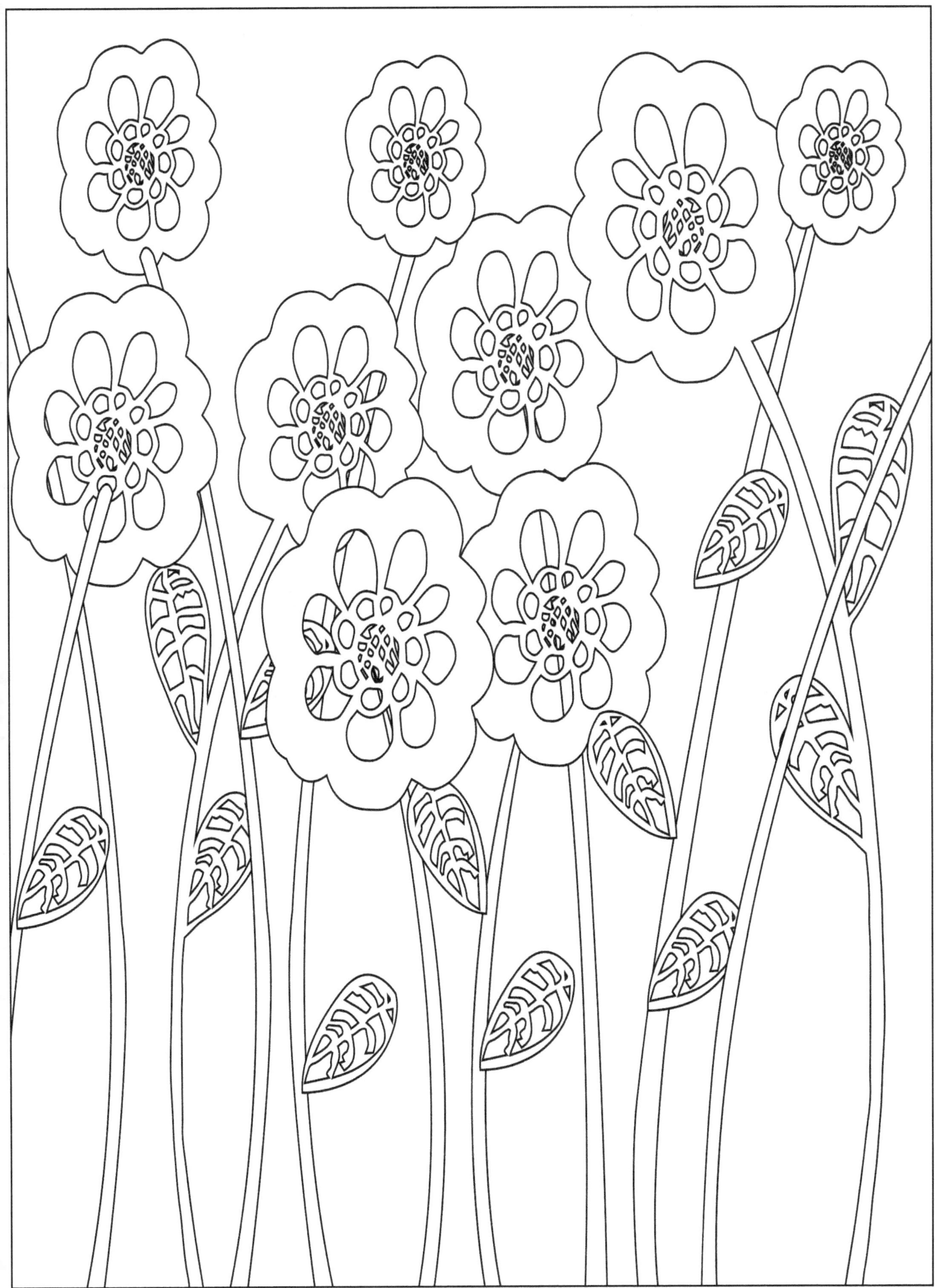

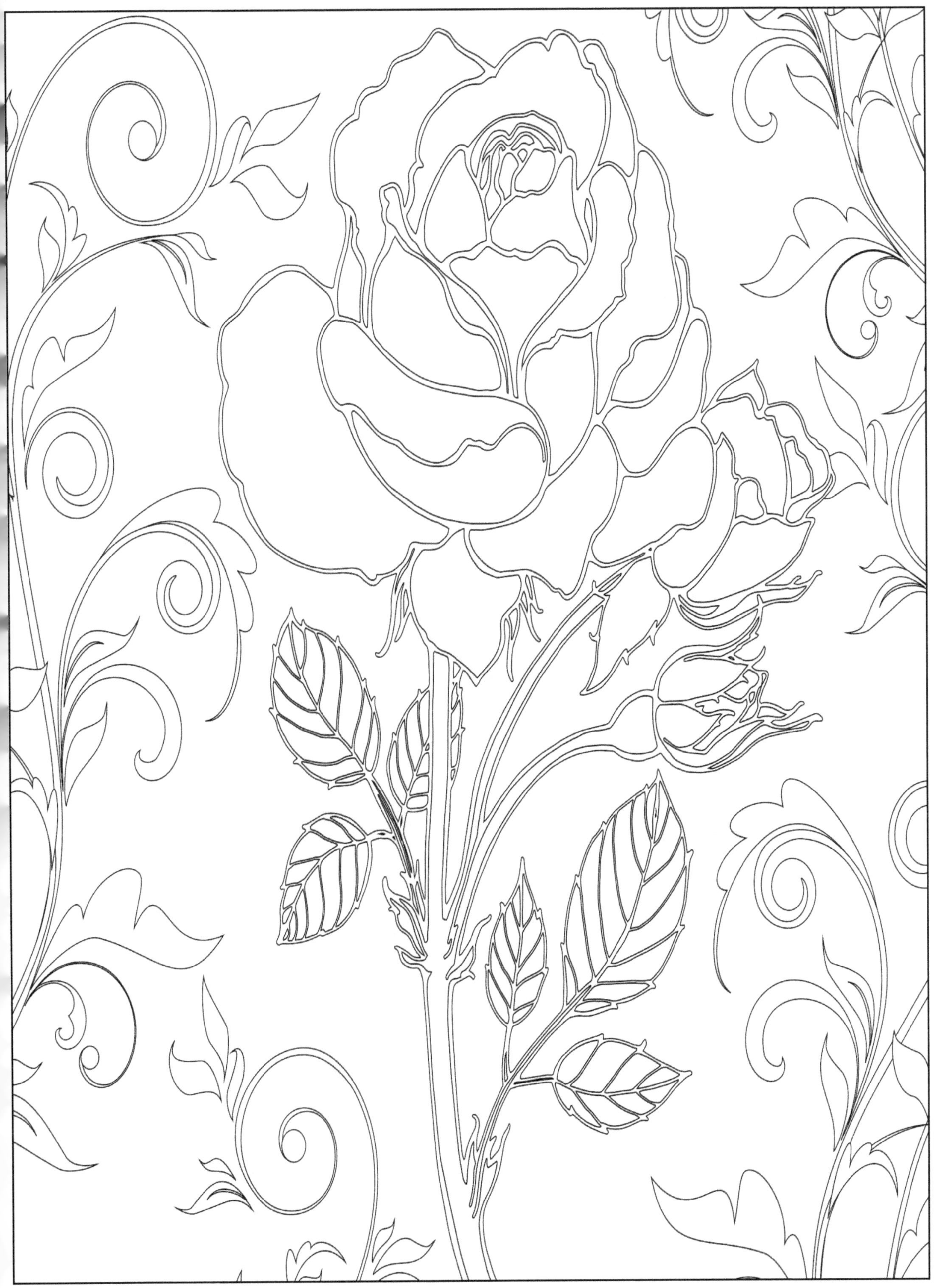